SUN AND WIND

T0351392

CLASSICS OF IRISH HISTORY
General Editor: Tom Garvin

Original publication dates of reprinted titles are given in brackets

P. S. O'Hegarty, *The Victory of Sinn Féin* (1924)

Walter McDonald, *Some Ethical Questions of Peace and War* (1919)

Joseph Johnston, *Civil War in Ulster* (1913)

James Mullin, *The Story of a Toiler's Life* (1921)

Robert Brennan, *Ireland Standing Firm* and *Eamon de Valera* (1958)

Mossie Harnett, *Victory and Woe:*
The West Limerick Brigade in the War of Independence

Padraig de Burca and John F. Boyle, *Free State or Republic?*
Pen Pictures of the Historic Treaty Session of Dáil Éireann (1922)

Arthur Clery, *The Idea of a Nation* (1907)

Standish James O'Grady, *To the Leaders of Our Working People*

Michael Davitt, *Jottings in Solitary*

Oliver MacDonagh, *Ireland: The Union and its Aftermath* (1977)

Thomas Fennell, *The Royal Irish Constabulary:*
A History and Personal Memoir

Arthur Griffith, *The Resurrection of Hungary* (1918)

William McComb, *The Repealer Repulsed* (1841)

George Moore, *Parnell and His Island* (1887)

Charlotte Elizabeth Tonna,
Irish Recollections (1841/47 as *Personal Recollections*)

SUN AND WIND

Standish James O'Grady

edited by
Edward A. Hagan

University College Dublin Press
Preas Choláiste Ollscoile Bhaile Átha Cliath

First published by University College Dublin Press, 2004

Introduction and notes © Edward A. Hagan 2004

ISBN 1-904558-11-9
ISSN 1383-6883

University College Dublin Press
Newman House, 86 St Stephen's Green
Dublin 2, Ireland
www.ucdpress.ie

Cataloguing in Publication data
available from the British Library

Typeset in Ireland in Baskerville by Elaine Shiels, Bantry, Co. Cork
Printed on acid-free paper in Ireland by ColourBooks, Dublin

CONTENTS.

INTRODUCTION.

Edward A. Hagan

After Standish James O'Grady (1846–1928) died, one of his three sons, Hugh Art O'Grady, published *Standish James O'Grady: the Man and the Writer* in 1929. As its title suggests, the book reviews O'Grady's life and work. The son reports therein that his father was working on "Arcadia" when he died. Hugh Art's son, Standish DeCourcey O'Grady, preserved the typescript, edited in his grandfather's hand, of "Arcadia". It is a chapter in the book-length work, most of which is published here for the first time under O'Grady's title, *Sun and Wind*.

As the final testament of the "Father of the Irish Literary Renaissance" (an honorary title popularised by Ernest A. Boyd),[1] *Sun and Wind* offers insight into the intellectual history of Ireland from the mid-nineteenth century until O'Grady's death in 1928. *Sun and Wind* includes chapters published as journal articles as early as 1911 but later revised for inclusion in the book-length work. It is consistent with O'Grady's thinking after 1900 in which he writes very much under the influence of the anarchist and socialist ideas of thinkers such as Charles Fourier, Prince Peter Alekseyevich Kropotkin, and Henry George. O'Grady's later writing seems to contradict his earlier allegiance to his social class, the landlords of Ireland. However, it is well to note that O'Grady's early writing was usually highly critical of his own class, often upbraiding Ascendancy class landlords for decadence. O'Grady wrote for progressive publications after 1900 such as *The Peasant and Irish Ireland, The Irish Nation and the Peasant, The Irish Review, The New Age*, and *The Irish Worker*. From 1900 to 1906 he edited and wrote most of the articles for the *All Ireland Review*; he used it as an organ to promote restitution by England for its over-taxation of Ireland during the nineteenth century.

Since O'Grady was at once a political polemicist, a creative writer, and a somewhat unusual historian (by today's standards), we find him involved in all of these roles in *Sun and Wind*. However, this utopian treatise also reveals the pervasive influence of classical scholarship upon the Irish intellectual life of the period. In addition to the famed classical scholar and historian, John Pentland Mahaffy, classical students at Trinity College during the mid-nineteenth century included Alfred Percival Graves, Edward Dowden, Thomas Rolleston, Oscar Wilde, and John Bagnall Bury, among others, including O'Grady; all of these went on to claim "niches in literary history".[2]

After arguing the necessity for drastic change in Ireland in its first part, *Sun and Wind* makes extensive use of classical Greece in Part II as a model for the Ireland of O'Grady's time. Like Mahaffy, O'Grady is confident that Greek history is not just similar to Irish history; it is the template of all history, *the* universal cyclical pattern, which completed a full cycle in early Greece. It is well to note that O'Grady's earliest education was classical and that he remained a faithful student of the classics throughout his life; *Sun and Wind* references several of the most important classical scholarly works of the nineteenth and early twentieth centuries. While O'Grady began as a divinity student at Trinity College in 1864 and eventually changed the focus of his studies to law, he did win the classical scholarship while there. In his introduction to Hugh Art O'Grady's book, Graves writes that O'Grady "surprised all of us would-be scholars in his class by the beauty of his Greek verse".[3]

Although he received his B.A. from Trinity in 1868, he continued his study of law thereafter (thus maintaining his association with Trinity) and was called to the bar in 1872. During this period he and the other future famous men of letters at Trinity, published a literary magazine, *Kottabos*, which featured their Latin and Greek poems, translations, and imitations. One of O'Grady's first published articles was an article in *Dublin University Magazine* on the merits of *Kottabos*.[4] His poem, "On Reading the Fragments of Early Greek Lyric Poetry", appeared in *Kottabos*, probably sometime between 1869 and 1874.

The poem introduces O'Grady's very early interest in *prehistoric* Greece—the precise focus of *Sun and Wind*. His speculations about the nature of prehistoric Arcadia especially became his prescriptions for an ideal Ireland. The poem frankly asserts the superiority of the fragments—certainly to the popular contemporary Victorian verse of Martin Farquhar Tupper whose verse was the epitome of trite moralising but also to "our best" which "can be/Nought but loose clouds" as opposed to the fragments' "Clear stars of song". O'Grady was very early possessed of the idea that the Ireland of his time was endangered by decadent British culture. His speaker assesses the bad poetry that is comparable to the sound of that contemptible instrument, the trombone:

> We have all Tupper—not one thunder-tone
> Hath ceased to bellow through the British sky,
> And ladies tell us that the great trombone
> Will sound again . . .

The fragments, on the other hand, are "Hand breadths of wondrous streams, joyous and free,/That leap and foam and flash, and have no peers." However "The law that bound the Israelites of old/Slays you, the firstlings of Apollo's fold." Blame for the decadence that accompanied Greek civilisation at its height (and implicitly the British Empire) thus falls on the Hebraising tendencies that Matthew Arnold was to declare the opponent of Hellenism in his 1882 treatise, *Culture and Anarchy*. In claiming a Semitic cause for the destruction of early Greek lyric poetry, O'Grady follows standard, nineteenth-century ethnology, which often used philology as the "science" that would unlock the Aryan past.[5] He was ever keen to assert what might have been in dispute: that the Irish, often depicted as simians in nineteenth-century British comic art, were Aryans. In *Sun and Wind* he asserts that the "right and natural feeling of our Aryan ancestors has been obscured in more modern Europe by the prevalence of Semitic fanaticisms" (p. 38 below). While his idea of those fanaticisms included Roman Catholicism, O'Grady's early immersion in classical studies led him to believe deeply in the power of philology to uncover the ancient Aryan secrets that could counteract such fanaticisms. Philology in Ireland in the nineteenth century was brought to bear specifically on the fragments of early Greek literature. Mahaffy's biographers, W. B. Stanford and R. B. McDowell, credit him with identifying a fragment of a lost play by Euripides, *Antiope*, in the *Flinders Petrie Papyri* in 1890 and trace his early interest in papyri to a letter of enquiry to the British Museum in 1870.[6] Stanford and McDowell also note that "Sir J. Gardner Wilkinson had presented a copy of his *Fragments of the hieratic papyrus at Turin* to the T.C.D. library in 1852."[7] O'Grady was associated with Trinity at a time when unearthing the early histories of societies was attracting much attention, often spurred on by archaeological discovery as was the case in Mahaffy's identification of the Euripides fragment.

O'Grady, however, was to approach early history with a far different predilection from Mahaffy. Indeed *Sun and Wind* is in many ways an explicit answer to Mahaffy's often-expressed preferences for Greek civilisation. O'Grady's focus on Arcadia and the mountain-dwelling[8] Dorian Spartans runs directly counter to Mahaffy's more traditional appreciation for Athenian civilisation. Unlike the civilised Athenians (or the contemporary British): "We [Irish, implicitly pre-historic] seem to know better, to have more in common with them [the Dorian Spartans] than with the great historic Greeks." (p. 119 below). Mahaffy looked to Athenian history for a model for Ireland; O'Grady saw Arcadian pre-history as the text most appropriate to Ireland's current state of development and as the ideal prescription for avoiding entry into history. Stanford and McDowell argue persuasively that Mahaffy's use of Greek history was as much a commentary on contemporary Ireland as it was on ancient Greece. Mahaffy was staunchly Unionist and anti-Catholic in his sympathies and actively engaged the Irish language movement in the most vituperative of terms.[9] Declaring the study of Irish to be worthless and the continuance of small nations[10] such as Ireland to be disastrous, he staunchly opposed Irish nationalism.

Sun and Wind could not more directly oppose Mahaffy's views: O'Grady, the anarchist, declared that Arcadia was the ideal of local village autonomy, that a loose configuration of independent "countries" was later corrupted by the dominance of the Greek city-states. *Sun and Wind* frequently notes that the Greek history being discussed occurred in locales as small as County Mayo. The Dorian Greeks, from whom Sparta sprang, lived in ideal small communities, still worthy of emulation in the twentieth century. He argues, for example: "Therefore, we need one of our vast rich Christian Irish Provinces to sustain a population equal in number to that which the little Heathen[11] Spartan Empire maintained in the days of Leonidas, and maintained in comfort and prosperity, in a condition of manly opulence and physical and moral efficiency" (p. 75 below).[12]

O'Grady turns Mahaffy's reasoning on its head and uses fragmentary knowledge of early Greek history to write his programme for Ireland. Like Mahaffy, however, O'Grady claimed to be able to fill in the missing history by using the truth of his imagination.

In doing so, O'Grady could look back to the lasting influence of the "father of scientific history", Barthold Georg Niebuhr (1776–1831), upon his work. O'Grady is most famous for his "bardic histories"—his two-volume *History of Ireland* published in 1878 and 1880. Far from being a "scientific" history of Ireland, the "bardic histories" tell the stories of the ancient semi-mythical heroes of Ireland—principally Cuchulain—for the first time in modern English. The two books launched the Irish Literary Revival; most revival writers acknowledged their debt to O'Grady. Yeats, for example, said, O'Grady's "'History of Ireland, Heroic Period' . . . started us all."[13]

O'Grady, however, believed that the bardic literature was actually based on early history whom redactors had embellished over the centuries. When he wrote his "bardic history", he had Niebuhr's *History of Rome* firmly in mind, for to "write a great and valuable history of Ireland, one should combine the science of Niebuhr and the imagination of Livy".[14] O'Grady was to repeat his indebtedness to Niebuhr's method on several occasions, and his "bardic histories" reflect his desire to use the method.

Niebuhr's three-volume *History of Rome* was written in German and revised between 1811 and 1832; it was translated into English by Tennyson's mentors at Cambridge, Julius Charles Hare and Connop Thirwall, between 1828 and 1842. Niebuhr's influence on historiography and Victorian thinking cannot be overstated: he has been called the father of scientific history. He used the new "science" of philology "to sever the poetical ingredients from what is historically sure and well-grounded".[15] What Niebuhr meant by the science of philology might not seem so scientific by today's standards; he had a very Romantic idea of philology as "science". John Edwin Sandys has described Niebuhr's view of the "high ideal of a scholar's life" and the proper training for it:

> The authors specially recommended for study are Homer, Aeschylus, Sophocles and Pindar, with Herodotus, Thucydides, Demosthenes and Plutarch, and Cicero, Livy, Caesar, Sallust, and Tacitus. All these were to be read with reverence, not with a view to making them the themes of aesthetic criticism, but with a resolve to assimilate their spirit. This (he declares) is the true 'Philology' that brings health to the soul, while learned investigations (in the case of such as attain to them) belong to a lower level.[16]

Niebuhr's *History of Rome* is famous for having "unmasked" Livy's patriotic goal of writing history to support his particular definitions of Roman patriotism. Niebuhr's history is the classic attempt to strip away the additions, distortions and modifications of the redactors of Roman history in order to recover the original *carmina* or songs that Niebuhr believed lay at the root of Rome's founding. Niebuhr believed strongly that, because he had absorbed "the true 'Philology' that brings health to the soul" he could recover the buried *fragments* of the original history.

Niebuhr further believed that Rome was more susceptible to this kind of enquiry because "the poems, out of which (in his view) 'the history of the Roman kings was resolved into a prose narrative'", knew "nothing of *the unity which characterises the most perfect of Greek poems* ".[17] Niebuhr thus believed that societies went through a kind of evolutionary development from the primitive to the highly civilised—as was the case in ancient Greece. O'Grady was strongly influenced by this idea to see in Ireland a prehistoric country dominated by a highly civilised country—England. This was not news, but for O'Grady it meant that Ireland might avoid English decadence if it would only understand its historical position. Yeats called the members of his group the "last Romantics"; O'Grady had a highly developed idea of what that Romanticism might mean. Thus his "bardic history" project was a scientific philological project to restore the Irish to their equivalent of the Roman *carmina*. O'Grady, like Niebuhr, believed in his ability to absorb the spirit of the ancient works.

Thus at the beginning of his career, O'Grady used the ancient Irish tales as the basis for his "bardic history". (Contrary to some views of his version, O'Grady "stripped down" the redactions and fanciful embellishments of the tales and, from his perspective, restored their historicity.) At the end of his career, O'Grady was preparing this book-length treatise on Greek prehistory—*Sun and Wind*—as his template for the ideal Ireland. O'Grady believed he could use the truth of his imagination to restore Greek pre-history as an object lesson for the Irish. Niebuhr had provided the model by his examination of Rome; O'Grady therefore argues with confidence that he is able to reconstruct that prehistory from "the vast Greek Epic cycle, now lost, known to us only from late Greeks who could only echo the echoes of the echoes of the great lost Epics" (p. 133 below).

While O'Grady does not mention Niebuhr in _Sun and Wind_, the influence is palpable. For example, O'Grady condemns the kind of history Mahaffy (among others) was writing, but significantly he chooses Roman history to make his point: "She is loud about the criminalities and insanities of imperial Rome, silent about the Ramnes Tities and Luceres, dumb about the times when the grand Roman character was being formed, eloquent about its corruption" (p. 123 below). Niebuhr devotes much of a chapter in his first volume—"The Beginning of Rome, and Its Earliest Tribes"—to a discussion of these three tribes, the Ramnes, Tities, and Luceres. And O'Grady could not have missed the fact that Niebuhr used "the Irish parliament till 1782" in that chapter as an example of how Roman institutions followed the same pattern of development as later European institutions.[18]

Now it is not likely that O'Grady would have been entirely pleased by Niebuhr's use of the Irish Parliament since O'Grady's utopian views were more anarchistic than Niebuhr's predilection for institutions as determining factors in history would have tolerated. Nevertheless, it is important to see that, like Niebuhr, O'Grady believed in an evolutionary pattern of the movement from prehistory to history. In that regard his thinking resembles Marxist and socialist ideas of history. However, the most likely source for this kind of evolutionary thinking was Charles Fourier (1772–1837), the French utopian socialist, of whom O'Grady says in _Sun and Wind_: "There is always something worth thinking of even in Fourier's most flagrant paradoxes" (p. 22 below). Fourier was an implacable foe of English industrial society and especially the theorists of modern capitalism, Adam Smith (1723–90), David Ricardo (1772–1832), and Thomas Malthus (1766–1834). Fourier argued that he had discovered the laws of passional attraction—a discovery on a par with Newton's discovery of the laws of physical attraction. The laws of passional attraction established the absolutely scientific basis for the ideal community, or phalanx: it would have exactly 1620 people equally distributed by gender—exactly twice the 810 varieties of human passions that he claimed to have defined. O'Grady is silent about these passions although he clearly knows that Fourier is odd. Nevertheless, O'Grady believes that the pre-historic Dorian Greeks, from whom the Spartans emerged, lived in communities of comparable size. Whenever the communities threatened to become too large, a new community would be formed by willing explorers from the fully grown community; thus a perfect society could be maintained. O'Grady is not shy in claiming categorically to know the truth of such organisation: "The Greeks are the grand champions and representatives in history of the idea of the small State and its realisation in practice" (p. 124 below).

In that stage of history, virtue abounded. Thus O'Grady, unlike Mahaffy and other Athenian partisans, admires Spartan virtue while wondering about the value of Athenian civilisation. And he is not slow to make the modern point that surely would have pleased Fourier:

> the great English character was never formed in these late centuries of commercialism and Empire. Rather, England is today living upon and consuming something accumulated in times pre-historic or extra-historic, just as Greece in those blazing centuries of her glory, the 5th. and 4th. B.C., used up, dissipated, squandered, a wealth of human power and virtue which had been slowly accumulating through millenniums of which history knows nothing (p. 65 below).

Of course, O'Grady is confident that he can inform us of that history. He, like Niebuhr, never seems to have seen that he might be accused of falling into the very trap of the redactors he was trying to undo. (Today, O'Grady's "bardic history" is regarded as just another redaction.) Instead, like Fourier, he confidently attacks Adam Smith's view of the laws of economics by reference to the inexorable progress of trade:

for O'Grady this led to enslavement of the weak, except that in Sparta, because of its virtue, such contact with outside traders was banned.

And clearly in *Sun and Wind* O'Grady is striving to keep the Irish free from the traders and the dissipation that accompanies contact with them. His late additions to the text reveal his pessimism about the prospects for the Irish. In fact, he may even have been influenced by Bram Stoker's *Dracula* as in the typescript version he added the word "monstrous" to this description of the atrocious conditions of modern society:

> But something has intervened, some unnatural monstrous thought, or desire grown passionate, furious, reckless of consequences, has compelled him to expel this great natural and divine love out of his heart, and to admit and cherish, in its stead, some other un-natural conflicting passion which drives him helpless into his dens, to mean and joyless labour there till the Sun sets (p. 7 below).

When he published his "Sun and Wind" chapter in *The New Age* in 1913, he proclaimed the Irish peasantry as the new type of Irish Hero. To this version he added several very pessimistic passages that reflect his belief that the monstrosity of a Dracula was now afoot: the peasants' time has passed: "This great Irish Order is failing to-day, and even failing fast" (p. 65 below). In his series of columns in *The Irish Worker* in 1912 and 1913—*To the Leaders of Our Working People*—O'Grady had tried to create a movement of Dublin city workers back to countryside communes that resemble Fourier's ideal. He seems in later years to have despaired of its realisation. Like Fourier, O'Grady was concerned to make work fun once again; modern industrial society had made it into stultifying drudgery.

For O'Grady modern industrial society was a comprehensive plot to enslave workers and destroy their innate innocence. Thus O'Grady's early chapters in *Sun and Wind* establish the need to look to Greek history because of the destruction of virtue by the confinement of youth indoors in cities as opposed to the unfettered life of the country. O'Grady, whose books include two commercially successful boys' stories, argued most directly in *To the Leaders of Our Working People* that school ruined boys. *Sun and Wind* claims that there was no need for written laws or literacy at all in ancient Sparta because the laws "were alive, in men's hearts. No one in the Empire was able to read or write" (p. 106 below). In fact, O'Grady seems to have believed that the creative process by which ideal communities are established in pre-history was recapitulated in the individual lives of boys, who might develop as individuals the virtue characteristic of the entire community by avoiding the kind of literacy that comes with indoor schooling. He argues that it is futile to attempt to control young boys; to do so is to warp their creative urges into violent urges. Instead, we need to see that ". . . Man is born a warrior, but . . . the war to which he is born is a divine war, not an infernal. Then his thinkers and teachers must let him loose there. Once shown the way and the goal of it and let loose there he will go like a—hurricane, and as uncontrollably" (p. 127 below). However, the context makes clear that, when so let loose, the results will be beneficent, not destructive.

O'Grady's words can quite easily be twisted to support notions of revolutionary anarchy, and he apparently never could see that his military metaphors could be manipulated to produce destructive violence. However, he saw that Spartan society was highly disciplined and not chaotic at all. And it should be noted that its hierarchical nature appealed to O'Grady, who as a member of the fallen Anglo-Irish Ascendancy class, seems always to have been looking for ways to re-establish an aristocratic class that would truly be the "aristoi", the "best".

O'Grady was surely worried that Irish society was just as likely to turn to its worst as to its best. Accordingly, in *Sun and Wind* it is clear that he decided to take on the forces in Irish society very directly that he was most concerned about. The most obvious of these targets is the Roman Catholic Church.

O'Grady, like Yeats, George Russell and other Irish and modernist writers, seems to have dabbled in occult systems. At one point he tells us, "Mind is everything, Matter nothing" (p. 74 below). Apparently some evidence exists that his wife may have been a medium. *Sun and Wind* reflects a mind that has assimilated at least some theosophical thinking. For example, Rosicrucians believe that religious progress occurs by an evolution backwards to previous optimal conditions. It is not hard to see how such a belief coincides with O'Grady's preference for pre-history. However, the Rosicrucian connection may be most clearly seen in O'Grady's use of the Vedas (presumably a document created by those in closest proximity to the wellspring of the Aryan "race") near the close of *Sun and Wind*. There he describes a young man making a milk-offering (p. 142 below). The practice resembles what Yeats presented in *The Land of Heart's Desire*, a play with strong Rosicrucian connections.[19] In that play backward evolutionary progress from Roman Catholicism empowers faeries or the preceding deities of Ireland by the protagonist's giving of milk to them.

    Sun and Wind in many respects attempts to reconstruct Irish Catholicism. O'Grady alludes to the prevalent Protestant theological idea that the age of miracles was over ("the gleaming dawn of history when anything might have happened" (p. 78 below) —a rationalist explanation for the absence of miracles in the centuries succeeding Biblical times. Such a position hardly squares with official Roman Catholic acknowledgement of the continuance of miraculous happenings such as cures and apparitions. Similarly O'Grady identifies the creation of idols and images with the decline of religion—traditional Protestant charges against Catholic practices—and the emergence of the Greeks into history: "The genius of the Greek was failing when he made marble men and called them Gods" (p. 78 below). Instead O'Grady characterises Greek religious practice as healthy when it resembles druidical practices: then their symbols of their Gods were "still mostly an-iconic, that is, formless undefined symbols of the Gods" (p. 78 below). Then,

. . . the people who worshipped the bit of oak or ash or pine, calling it their Father, Friend, Captain and Protector, singing loud and clear their choral songs, were better, braver, purer and nobler by far, by very far, than the highly civilised, cultured and cultivated people who, in the great temple of Olympian Zeus on the banks of the Alpheus, worshipped, or thought they worshipped, the august, unsurpassed figure carved by Pheidias to be the wonder of the whole world (p. 114 below).

Analysis of O'Grady's rhetoric reveals that he is quite deliberately using the Roman Catholic language of Mary's sympathy to describe Nature (p. 42 below). Similarly he tells the story of the origin of the Arcadians in touching language that suggests the origin of worship of the Lady: "The children knew then why they went in procession once a year to Mount Lyceum, and why they made sacrifices on the altar of Arcas, and why they worshipped someone named Despoina or the Lady" (pp. 100–1 below). O'Grady, like his friend George Russell, seems to want to transfer Catholic religious fervour back to pre-historic nature worship in the manner of the druids. O'Grady does not seek to make Catholics into Protestants as he openly questions the value of the Christian idea of Eden: "not the poor confined Paradise which was imagined by the Semitic child-mind of the Orient . . ." (p. 52 below). Instead he champions a more pagan idea of Paradise. Similarly, he speaks of the secular poet Robert Burns as an "unordained" clergyman (p. 32 below)—a prevailing idea expressed most directly by Coleridge that the idea of the clergy had to be broadened to include new kinds of spiritual leaders. He even gives great credence to the rather bizarre religious calculations of Francis Dobbs, who used numerological strategies and claimed that he had received direct spiritual information from the source itself.

O'Grady most directly attacks Catholicism by reference back to the Inquisition and its practice of issuing "auto-da-fes" (p. 49 below). Use of the word with its direct reference to the decrees of the Spanish Inquisition makes clear that O'Grady is attacking the authority of the Roman Catholic Church. At no other time in his career has O'Grady been so outspoken in his opposition to Catholicism. His text is loaded with allusions to the King James version of the Bible; no Catholic ear could fail to recognise whose Bible O'Grady is quoting. In proposing his utopia at the end of his life, O'Grady seems to have taken the gloves off with reference to Catholicism in particular, and Christianity in general, for the King James allusions usually serve to show that Christian religious belief has its origin in prehistoric religious practice. In fact, he is not kind to the pre-Christian British either: at one point O'Grady argues that ox sacrifice grew up in the decadence of Greek religion; he leaves it to the reader to know that pre-Christian Anglo-Saxon religious practice was characterised by ox sacrifice (p. 145 below). We may confidently presume that O'Grady thought worship grew more decadent once the Anglo-Saxons came to power in England and Christianity arrived.

O'Grady reveals himself as a thoroughly modern writer in his belief that the old ways had failed and that the writer must be a new kind of cleric, preaching a vastly different salvation. The available evidence suggests that from 1918 to 1928 he lived mostly with his son, Carew James Standish. They are both listed on the voting rolls in Easton Maudit in Northamptonshire in 1925, where Carew was given the living by the Marquess of Northamptonshire. Carew had been ordained in Ireland upon completing his training at the Church of Ireland seminary at Meath after graduating from Trinity. Carew may have had a significant influence on his father's thinking. Carew spent his early career (1917–21) in English public schools (Merchant Taylor's in London and Chigwell in Essex, to name two) as both chaplain and science teacher—a combination of interests that suggests that Carew may have been a progressive sort of clergyman. It is true that O'Grady seems to have become greatly concerned about environmental issues and seems to talk about Nature in a way that suggests more than a classicist's acquaintance with a scientific understanding of it. The very title, *Sun and Wind*, suggests that O'Grady had become a modern ecologist. O'Grady expresses very progressive views of Christian thinking and is given to seeing all religious practice as similar, evidencing human creativity.

Sun and Wind also reveals a secular progressive O'Grady, who seems to support the idea of the New Woman. He seems to be consciously referencing stereotypical, negative ideas of the New Woman: "She loved nothing, nor anyone. Wonderfully, miraculously gifted otherwise, she had no heart or soul" (p. 44 below). However, he does so in order to reject such ideas as nonsense and to suggest that Nature is feminine and Love itself.

In 1875 O'Grady became the first European to publish a full-length article[20] in appreciation of Walt Whitman, whom he saw as the harbinger of the evolution of society towards a new and hopeful age of the common man as hero. At the same time O'Grady was deeply influenced by the writings of Thomas Carlyle, who railed against the democratising influence of America, most notably in his 1867 essay, "Shooting Niagara—And After?" In *Sun and Wind* we find a similar paradoxical mixture of ideas. We should not be tempted to "iron out" the complexity of this thinking by keeping him in the box of spokesman for the dying Anglo-Irish power structure. *Sun and Wind* reflects a mind not so easily categorised. We need to attend to it.

NOTES.

1 *Ireland's Literary Renaissance.* (New York: John Lane, 1918).

2 W. B. Stanford and R. B. McDowell, *Mahaffy: A Biography of an Anglo-Irishman* (London: Routledge & Kegan Paul, 1971), p. 44.

3 Alfred Percival Graves, "Foreword", in Hugh Art O'Grady, *Standish James O'Grady: The Man and the Writer* (Dublin and Cork: Talbot, 1929), p. 10.

4 Standish James O'Grady [Arthur Clive], "*Kottabos*", *Dublin University Magazine* 84 (1874), pp. 565–79.

5 For more discussion of the Aryan myth in Ireland in the nineteenth century, see Edward A. Hagan, "The Aryan Myth: A 19th Century Anglo-Irish Will-to-Power?" in Tadhg Foley and Sean Ryder (eds), *Ideology and Ireland in the Nineteenth Century* (Dublin: Four Courts, 1998), pp. 197–205.

6 Stanford and McDowell, *Mahaffy*, p. 183.

7 *Ibid.*, p. 252n.

8 The original Aryans were also thought to have been mountain-dwellers.

9 Mahaffy called the revival of Irish "a retrograde step, a return to the dark ages, to the Tower of Babel." Quoted by George Russell in Lady Gregory (ed.), *Ideals in Ireland* (London, 1901); quoted, in turn, by Stanford and McDowell in *Mahaffy*, p. 105.

10 Stanford and McDowell write: "As for Ireland's right to political freedom, the world was [according to Mahaffy], always had been, and always would be, better off without small, independent, nationalistic states. . . . From his early days as a scholar he had preferred the large Hellenistic kingdoms to the smaller city-states of classical Greece." *Mahaffy*, p. 123.

11 O'Grady inserted "Heathen" and "Christian" into the typescript upon revision—evidence that he wished to question the value of Christianity.

12 Because of its preference for the pre-Christian Heathens and its use of masculine idealisations, O'Grady may be alluding to Nietzsche's idea of the Superman (*Also Sprach Zarathustra*, 1891) in this sentence.

13 W. B. Yeats, quoted in George Russell [AE], "The Dramatic Treatment of Heroic Literature", *Samhain* (Oct. 1902), p. 12.

14 Standish James O'Grady [Arthur Clive], "Irish Archaeology", *Dublin University Magazine* 88 (1876), p. 650.

15 Barthold Georg Niebuhr, *The History of Rome*, tr. Julius Charles Hare and Connop Thirlwall (London: Taylor, Walton & Maberly, 1851), vol. I, p. xvii.

16 John Edwin Sandys, *A History of Classical Scholarship*, vol. 3, (Cambridge: Cambridge University Press, 1903–8), p. 80.

17 *Ibid.*, p. 78.

18 Niebuhr, *History of Rome*, vol. I, p. 300.

19 For a discussion of the Rosicrucian practices in Yeats's play, see Hagan, "The Aryan Myth: An Anglo-Irish Will-to-Power?", pp. 204–5.

20 "Walt Whitman, the Poet of Joy", *The Gentlemen's Magazine* 85 (1875), pp. 513–32.

A NOTE ON THE TEXT.

The available evidence suggests that *Sun and Wind* was composed and compiled between 1911 and 1928. The type-script bears evidence of several apparently abortive attempts to put it together as a book. O'Grady did divide it into two parts and assigned conflicting chapter numbers that reflect more than one ordering plan. I have assigned chapter numbers here to reflect the ordering that makes the most sense of O'Grady's plans as they evolved over such an extended period of time. In fact, one page is slightly burned and then O'Grady's hand-writing around the burn mark suggests that he himself may have rescued it from the fire. It seems to have been written both before and after the First World War as it hints at the doom about to descend upon Europe. (O'Grady's son, Standish Conn, was an ace in the British Flying Corps during the war.) On the other hand, O'Grady makes apparent reference to living in England very early on in the text: "Here, out of Ireland, in the light of the great ascending Sun, I declare that the civilisation which drives men to do such things, and, which blinds them as to their horror, is impious, unnatural, and accurst; I say that this civilisation is going to perish; surely" (p. 6 below). Such reference seems to come from the period of residence—*c.* 1918–28—with his son, Carew. His description of armies seems also to reflect a consciousness of the results of war and is thus a post-war statement: ". . . mutual fratricide, and the creation of widows and orphans and cripples" (p. 8 below).

The typescript with corrections and additions, principally in O'Grady's hand, was preserved by Standish DeCourcey O'Grady; it was arranged in an order and with chapter notations (omitted here because they are too confusing) that suggest that it was being prepared for book publication. A copy of one chapter, "Arcadia", is part of the Jeanne R. Foster–William M. Murphy Collection of Irish and Anglo-Irish Miscellanea, which now is housed in the New York Public Library, in the Manuscripts and Archives Division. The Foster–Murphy provenance suggests that this chapter was probably given at some time to the collector, John Quinn, as were other O'Grady documents in the New York Public Library.

This version contains all of the handwritten corrections found in the Standish DeCourcey O'Grady Collection as well as other corrections that suggest a later revision for the version in the New York Public Library. Therefore I have used this later version to prepare *Sun and Wind* for publication here. I am indebted to Standish DeCourcey O'Grady, William M. Murphy, and the New York Public Library for permission to use these typescripts.

PART I.

SUN AND WIND.

ONE.

AN IRISH SUNRISE.

And God said, let there be light, and there was light
And God saw that the light was good.

(Genesis 1: 3–4.)

I write these lines on the side of our Wicklow Mountains
looking eastward over the Irish Sea beyond which, faintly
outlined, the Welsh Hills swim in mist. Beyond those quiet
hills, unseen but un-forgotten, for who can ever forget him?—
the great industrial English giant, roused by his hooting sirens,
is just now awaking, to renew his endless labour. The mad
Titan! Raging amid his huge industries, and beset by problems
huger than his industries! As I look, I seem to hear again, this
transparent dewy morning, what in the great cities of England,
I have heard so often in the black and dark night, that fierce,
insistent, heart-torturing hoot, and hoot, and hoot again of his
sirens shouting for him to come, "work"; and, afterwards, the
thunder of his million-footed armies rushing to battle. To
battle! With whom? Or with what? Or Why? Or to what end?
Why are those mad millions rushing to battle, those wild
sirens hooting—all in the dewy morning?

The Sun, not a foot above the horizon, lets me gaze my
fill, with undazzled eyes at his glowing disc. His intolerable
meridian brightness is still veiled by the Morning.

I saw him set last night; saw him set, yet no night succeeded.
Sol occubuit; nox nulla secuta est.[1]

Through the few fragrant twilight hours of the Monarch's absence he let us know that he was not far away. We saw the light-banners of his radiant host borne round the northern horizon where he travelled, he and his armies, eastward, ever eastward, to the scene of his new red birth and dirurnal glorious avatar.

Sol invictus! The unconquered sun!

Why should Man choose one day out of the seven and call it his, when every one of them is his already? Is he not the daily creator of the day? Every day is the sun's day.

Through those few hours of luminous shadow there was silence; and, yet not silence; for the grouse were talking with each other in the heather, and the night-jar reeling, for ever reeling, as he wheeled; beautiful unseen singing creature! heard by all, seen by none. And at midnight, a reed-warbler sang; and always, our little mountain streams kept tinkling, playing with liquid tender fingers upon their stony lyres. I distinguished the separate notes of three of them; the sweet innocents! And, twice, the cheerful cock announced to the World that "all" was "well"; and distant dogs barked: "Ware thief! I, the dog, am here. I am on guard." Then the glad lark soared, singing, from his bed in grass or heather, and the early crow, intent on breakfast, flew croaking past; and the brave blackbird and the cheerful thrush awoke and lifted up their voices and shouted their grand bravuras.

Then, the miraculous Dawn, so heralded, so welcome by glad singing pouring forth, out of millions of innocent throats, the beautiful bird populations of the Earth—so heralded. Dawn, the silver-skirted, silent, swift advanced, without sound, out of the Orient, in her beauty, and stripped the shy earth bare, and unshadowed the world; sending out before her, her own millions and octillions of avant couriers clad in pearly grey. The beautiful, beautiful Dawn! the ever pursued but never captured Dawn! for ever bride, but for ever virgin bride of the pursuing Sun: type, for ever, of the loveliest thing that the World knows; girlhood, its sweetness, beauty, purity and goodness!

Girls of Ireland, beautiful daughters of the Dawn, will you help me? For I know that you can save us, save the World and liberate Mankind; if you will. I shall tell you, clearly "how", in due time. For I see in you the great prophecy fulfilled; the Hero born of Woman and His heel on the neck of the Serpent. Remember and don't fail me.

And, as the Dawn passed westward, scattering the blanket of the dark, stripping Ireland bare, reaching out beyond Ireland, out westward over the great Atlantic, then, suddenly, the flaming cause of all that vanguard of music and beauty, alike that of the dim mysterious night and of the silver-skirted fleeing Dawn, the flaming cause of it all arose in his glory, and looked benignantly upon his world, pouring forth over all his creatures, insect, and bird, and beast, and Man, over all things animate and inanimate, the boundless floods of his light and fire, and charging for it, not one penny, not a cent. The warm light falls everywhere: over England's huge and monstrous Cities, over this gleaming Channel, over Ireland's vast savannahs, following the Dawn over the Atlantic, silent everywhere. And, just as quietly and impartially, the vast light which encloses half the Planet, this lovely warm light falls upon the little sheet of white paper on which I write; on which I try to set down in stammering prose some weak echo of that half-heard strong Hymn of love and praise, which, if I could, I would so gladly utter, and with a full throat in thy honour, O most mighty, unfathomable living fountain of Light and Fire. Yet, who of men can praise thee rightly, praise thee at all in times like these? when the Nations, each in proportion to its imagined greatness, have conspired to despise thee, seeking with curtains of clay and stone to exclude thy blessed light, and hide themselves from thy vital ray. Obsessed, night-mare driven, insane! who grope for wealth in the dark, and for happiness in obscure dens.

The wild seer of the Apocalypse, in his vision of the coming of the great Judge and Avenger, saw the Nations fleeing from his presence, heard them calling upon the rocks and the mountains to cover them. But we, actually and with our eyes,

see something more wonderful. We see great Nations, not
alarmed by the coming of any judge and avenger, not as yet,
laboriously concealing themselves from the loveliest and the
gentlest and the most life-giving thing that we know; which is
the light. We see them rushing, panic-stricken, into their dens
and hiding-places, seeking shelter everywhere, anywhere,
provided only that they may, so, be able to escape from the
light of thy glorious face, O, Sun. And they call to each other,
encouragingly, hoping by their loud clamour to subdue, a
little, the universal terror:

"Come! Hasten! It is day. Let us go down into the Earth, in
our millions, into the holes that we have digged. Let us, in our
millions, go into our smoke-bebannered tall factories, and
serve well our iron demons there. Let us, in our millions, go
into our dim traps and Offices, and turn on our artificial lights
there, and worship well there our great god, Mammon. He
will save us; a few of us."

Here, out of Ireland, in the light of the great ascending
Sun, I declare that the civilisation which drives men to do such
things, and, which blinds them as to their horror, is impious,
unnatural, and accurst; I say that this civilisation is going to
perish; surely. I say that Nature meant Man to live in the
Light, that he ought to live in the Light, and that he knows
that he ought. He knows that when the Sun rises and he
himself leaves his couch, refreshed with slumber and when he
crosses the threshold of his home, Nature never meant him to
go indoors again into an office or a shop or a factory, or down
in to a mine, and spend the bright day there.

You know that I am speaking the truth.

Everything that lives loves the Light, some very few things
excepted, which Nature, for her own good reasons, has made
nocturnal; such as bats and moles, things of twilight and the
dusk. They, in evading the Light, follow loyally the law of
their being. Man is not one of them. He belongs to the order
of things that delight in the Day and rejoice in the Sun.
Excepting those few nocturnal things, all creation delights in
the Light. The flowers open their hearts to the Sun, and for

him pour forth their sweetness. The trees—why, they are embodied sunlight, the Sun's fire miraculously transmuted. See the trees hewn, divided, and on the hearth; how the imprisoned flame which, through their myriad green leaves, they once drank in at that fountain of fire—how it shoots forth, filling the home with kindly warmth and gay light, like a captured and escaping god; which perhaps it is. Perhaps it is. When the little-Greek child heard the kindled timber crackling on the hearth, he used to cry:

"Listen! Hephaistos is laughing."

Our own children, to whom the romance of life and such Nature-poetry are forbidden, cannot be prevented from being happy in the morning at the incoming of the Light, and happy round the quivering flames of the hearth, the quivering, shivering, appealing, Love—making flames of the Hearth.

Earth and Ocean rejoice in the Sun. The Earth, like a bride, unveils all her beauty for him, her lord and lover. The Sea, smit by his ray, shines and lightens: Ocean's myriad wavelets laugh and dance before him, like the young naked ecstatic David before the Ark.

Why does man, only, flee from him, and, at his coming, bury himself in dens of brick and stone? Why?

He loves the Sun, surely; Nature has so made him that he must. Love of the Light is born in him. But something has intervened, some unnatural monstrous thought, or desire grown passionate, furious, reckless of consequences, has compelled him to expel this great natural and divine love out of his heart, and to admit and cherish, in its stead, some other un-natural conflicting passion which drives him helpless into his dens, to mean and joyless labour there till the Sun sets. Then, when the Sun sets, he is free. When the Sun sets, he comes out again, he and the bat; Man and the beatle, and the bat.

He cannot help it; some demon is driving him. Who or what is that demon? Look around and consider.

What is it that Man loves and worships more than he loves the Sun? Is it not something which, like the Sun, is round, a disc? and which resembles the Sun, somewhat, as to its colour? It wears the hue of the crocus and of the daffodil, while it is not alive like them, or, like them, fragrant, and while, unlike those transitory fair daughters of the Sun, it is always in bloom. It is deader than the idols of old; but like the idols of old, it, too, has a certain deadly power. It can drive men, by millions, under the Earth, and, by millions, into factories, offices, and shops. It whips the little child indoors out of the Light, and chains to his desk the powerfully built athlete in the prime of life, and the grey haired veteran of sixty. See the millions of its slaves, respectable black-coated decoy slaves, bowed over their desks, the Planet over, chained to their desks as securely as ever were galley slaves to their oars.

And it can make Murder respectable too, this all-but Almighty god; respectable and also glorious. See how it feeds, clothes, and trains other millions, the best human material it can get, the young and the brave and the intelligent and the loyal; and equips them with the costliest and most terrible engines of destruction, and drives them on to mutual fratricide, and the creation of widows and orphans and cripples.

It is the God of the Earth; literally so. Money! What other God is, or ever was, able to do such things? Then, too, it is an absurd God, the absurdest that men, in their madness, ever bowed down before and worshipped. You can take this God and spin him under the table with your thumb and forefinger! and he will spin! You can put him in your pocket and take him out again, and lay him on a counter, and he will stay there, till he is removed—this God of the whole Earth; terrible heir of all the old tartarean and infernal gods and demons, devils and idols, of old time.—

And I want you, young men of Ireland, you before the rest, to begin the inevitable war against this brutal all-but Almighty God of the whole Earth. Face him and he will flee before you: nay, face him and he will vanish! For he is, at the same time, all-but Almighty, and—nothing! a phantom, a figment of the imagination of Man. Somewhere, upon the round Earth, this inevitable holy war, divine strife, this latest and greatest and last of all Crusades will begin. I want it begun in Ireland, my own country, land of the Heroes and the Saints: in the Isle of Destiny; Inis Fail. For I think that Destiny with its whips and scourges and inflicted sufferings and punitory and purgatorial preparations, has better equipped us than the rest to take the lead here and begin the great Exodus. You especially, young men and women of Ireland, boys and girls of Ireland, my appeal is chiefly to you. And I want you who are not young, and who for different reasons cannot share in that war, to arm and equip the young for the strife. I shall tell you how before I have done.

My young host—he is only nineteen,—emerges now from his hut, wearing his nocturnal loose pyjamas, a towel flung over his shoulder, and a big sponge in his hand. With a gay salutation to this scribbler he stalks up the hillside to enjoy his morning bath, where he has deepened, widened, and lined with concrete, a little natural pool made by one of the streamlets which I heard tinkling through the night.

Some one has made him a present of this bit of the Wicklow Highlands, and here he has built himself certain huts, not indeed astonishing forms of architecture, though I tell him that the Parthenon began with something like this; but good enough for youngsters like him, having some hardy Spartan fibre in their composition. I have myself slept soundly and well in one of them.

To my young host his small mountain estate, of some thirty acres, is little more than a toy, a place to spend holidays in, and his habitat just a lodge whence he sallies forth to slay the speckled trout in lake and river, while the pure sweet air purges the City soot out of his lungs.

I long to expand before him a vision of the great things that he might do—he and his friends; if they only would. But I dare not. He would not understand. The world and the world's God have been before me and preoccupied the ground.

When I was a young barrister and in daily attendance at the Four Courts in Dublin, I remember how my coevals and myself, not yet broken to that yoke, used to fume and fret, and kick vainly against the pricks. Sometimes when the beautiful sunlight streamed down on us through the glass roof of the Library, one of us would say to the rest:

"Well, boys, is it not a sin to be here on a day like this?"

And some one would reply: "Ay, it is that," the while he expanded his borrowed brief and dipped his quill in the inkpot.

And it was a sin surely; and is: a sin against Nature, and a deadly sin. And we dimly suspected the same, but believed ourselves powerless to resist the great Necessity which drove us on, gay delusions out in front of us and fierce whips behind.

My young host, still a student, is aiming towards one of those respectable callings, all of which conduct young men indoors and keep them there.

He would not understand me were I to talk to him as I do here. He would set me down as "cracked", or having "a bee in my bonnet"; and the parents and the sisters and the cousins and the aunts would never forgive me for attempting to put "such foolish notions into the boy's mind."

And you who read, and cannot at first understand, please remember that ever since you were six years old and even before, the God of the world has been teaching you, and deceiving you and compelling you to trust him and to despise the Power that made you. Remember that you are reading me through spectacles steeped in a solution of gold! If to-day you could see things as they are it would be a miracle.

From the Lowlands now a little rustic procession crosses the field before me on their way up to the mountains; they are a shepherd, his little grandson, Dannie, and a handsome intelligent sheepdog, called Point. The shepherd is 72 years of age, but erect and hale, and walks with long strong steps. The little grandson is, I hear, a good scholar, and has, I know, a bright face.

"Good-morrow, Brady. Going to be a grand day."

"A grand day, thank God," replies the shepherd.

If it were raining cats and dogs, Brady would say:—

"A fine soft day, thank God."

And if it were tempestuous, he would say:—

"A fine blowy day, thank God."

And if snow were deep on the earth, he would say:—

"Fine seasonable weather, thank God."

For Brady is a primitive Irish peasant, not yet quite corrupted by civilisation, and his feeling towards Nature is religious. He will not abuse or use bad language about any kind of weather which it may please God to send. Where did he get this pious feeling towards Nature? Partly it is natural and instinctive. Partly it has to come to him by descent and tradition from his remote Pagan ancestors; from men to whom all Nature was something divine, spiritual, semi-human. Our philosophers call this state of mind "Animism".

Animism or not, it is also the state of mind of the poet. Wordsworth, for example, was a thorough-going Animist. But all poets are made much in the same way.

Now Brady did not get this religious feeling towards Nature from his professed religion, which is hostile to it. Our ancient literature is steeped in that feeling. The Irish heathen bard could not or would not say, for example: "And next day"—but, "Then when the sun rose flaming, from his red-flaming couch." Some such language seemed to him only decent when speaking of things so august. In all our prayer-books, liturgies, and hymn-books, you will not find a trace of this spirit. The primitive Israelites had it, indeed; a great deal of it; a great deal of that beautiful instinctive natural piety. Much of their Old Testament is steeped in it; but growing gloomy and fanatical they brought it into their Synagogues and quenched it there.

The real religion of Europe is of course the worship of the crocus-coloured Idol.[2] The professed religion came to us out of the Synagogue and out of the cities of the later decadent Greeks, and regards with hatred and fear all the things that God made and blessed, and declared to be "good."

TWO.

A LITTLE EPIC AND A SMALL HERO.

The generation of Man, as revealed by modern embryology, is a miracle surpassing every other in this miraculous world,— one, too, which seems to demand an almost religious silence. Two or three words, nevertheless, concerning this wonder.

From a speck, out of something that is all but nothing, a mere potentiality in space and time, from a mysterious atom, mysteriously impregnated, vitalised, Nature creates and lavishly endows the strange being whom she means to be a Man. But before he sees the Light, she wills him, for reasons, to repeat the cosmic lesson which she has taught him, to go over again within the brief period of a few waxing and waning moons, all his cyclic aeonian experiences with her, to tell again the great story. She leads him through countless grades of known, unknown, unknowable existence until he has repeated the whole of his Planetary history, no phase of the same forgotten. Then and not till then is she ready to bring her man-child into the Light—her marvellous creation, the man-child, fully equipped, prepared for birth. And through all those ascending grades of being his still unconscious life-force has been ever instinctively blended with hers, obediently, loyally following her guidance and leading: Nature and Man being still, as it were, one. And the grand interest of childhood, an interest profoundly felt and profoundly expressed by the very Founder of our European religion, is this, that during the years of innocence, Nature and Man, the Mother and the child, are not indeed quite one as in those nine moons between birth and generation, but still quite undivorced. In his childhood Man and Nature are still in unrestrained comradeship, loving interdependence and glad co-operation, while they seem to exist in each other and through and for each other, like lovers: which they are. The separation is the Fall.

Let me tell in my own way the history of a child up to that moment when Sin and its twin, Sorrow, come upon the scene, and the Paradise recedes and is forgot. For the story of Paradise and the Fall is repeated today and every day.

In the sacred birth-processes, that strange divine tragedy which ends in laughter and happy tears, the infant Man is not passive; no; but valiantly co-operating and assisting. With all the strength that is in him he does what Nature herself directs and impels him to do. He strives and strains to be born. Nature wills him to be born; and he answers, all he can: "I will; I will be born."*

Born—she bids him breathe; draw his first breath of her holy air. She has made it for him, and him for it, having established between him and all her world a preordained harmony. She bids him breathe. With all his might, all the already considerable muscular power at his command, he struggles to breathe, every nerve of lungs, throat, diaphragm, brought to bear in the fulfilment of the gigantic task; struggles and strains: and succeeds! He takes his first breath, and, for the first time, lifts up his small voice; for she does not mean him to be amongst the number of her dumb creatures, but of her articulate.

She bids him see; see first of all her blessed Light. She made the Light for him and him for the Light. He obeys: looks intently with fixed gaze upon the Light, whether of

* O'Grady's note: Note, as we pass, that the same maternal divine Being who willed us to be born wills us also to die; and be assured that when the hour comes, we maugre all our silly shrinkings and apprehensions [and] will be found loyally co-operating, assisting all we can in great detachment; and, still obedient to her will, as eager to die as we were then to be born. While you are young, well and strong live in the assurance of this faith. You will find it solve many problems.

lamp or candle or, best of all, the good sunshine streaming in through the window; and, in that moment, learns, too, his first lesson in metaphysics, the difference between the Ego and the non-Ego, subject and object, the perceiver and the perceived, between Man and the world which surrounds him. But a very small dose of physics are enough for him, and the known results of that study immediately ensue. He falls fast asleep. She bids him sleep; he obeys and sleeps; and as he sleeps, breathes: practising ceaselessly the art which she has just taught him, and which no one else could have taught him but her.

Note that everything she has bidden him do has been for his good—to strain towards birth, to breathe her quickening air, to lift up his voice, to gaze on her wonderful light, to sink into slumber's soft receiving arms. And he, on his side, has been loyal and obedient, and in that obedience has begun to move forward in the direction of knowledge and power and the fulfilment of the whole purpose for which he was created. Then that straight-forward advance from knowledge to knowledge and from power to power he will maintain till the hour when the shadows begin to fall, when they, that is we, teach him, force him, over-persuade him to rebel. And the meaning of these chapters, indeed of this whole book, may be found here. Man is a failure upon the Earth, a blot on the fair face of creation solely because he is a rebel, refuses to be what Nature bids him be, to do what she bids him do, because he does that which she has commanded him not to do. For it is a dreadful mistake to imagine that Nature only prompts instincts, appetites, and passions. The vulgar think that, but you must not.

Awaking he is aware of the painful sensation called hunger and inanition. But his sweet Mother's breast awaits him, and well the little rascal knows how to deal with the same, Nature still teaching him, commanding him and he valiantly and with his whole heart responding. The words, inanition, gustation, and deglutition, are yet foreigners to this newly-arrived innocent tenderfoot, but he knows the things for which they stand as well as an alderman: better.

Have you ever observed that our words which we habitually employ are worlds removed from the things which they so arbitrarily represent: that our language, in fact, is as dead as a door-mat. We don't know why we say door or why we say mat. The language is dead. Our little hero whom we have just left taking his first drink will soon be calling a train, "puff-puff", because childhood loves vital speech if it can get it. I feel certain that our ancient Aryan ancestors used a language which was in all its parts alive and sparkling with significance. What a dead unlovely word is this, for example, which ends the foregoing sentence; but all our words are like it in this quality by deadness. Let me hazard a prediction; it is that when men begin to live again by returning to Nature they will strip these dead languages from their minds and tongues and create for themselves again a living speech. Man naturally hates all dead things, dead customs, institutions, dead religions, and dead words.

To return to the Hero of our small Epic—Nature wills him to become acquainted with the wonderful new world into which she has inducted him, which she has given to him as a birth present, and loyally and gladly he obeys. What his eyes see his hands go out to feel. He is correlating sight and touch; learning relative distances, the nature of space, what is far, what near, how some things are soft and some hard. Hour by hour, day by day he is learning, an apt delighted and obedient pupil making continual additions to his expanding stores of knowledge, his growing reservoir of mental and corporeal power, while all the time, lovingly cared for by the seen Mother, lovingly guided, assisted, and impelled to action by the unseen.

She means him to be not a selfish solitary but a lover of his kind, and gives him his sweet Mother, source of his daily nutrition, as his first beautiful human object of affection. From her breast looking up with milky lips he gurgles forth noises which translated mean:— "How nice you are! I love you." Nature bids him love, and he loves.

She means him to be articulate; may be, for the future is veiled, intends in him some grand orator or great baritone.

Hear him crowing lustily like chanticleer in the morning, delighted with the noise that he makes and with himself as the maker of it. Hear him singing thoughtfully a song all his own. It is said that at some time in our aeonian past our speech was song only when we lived in a universe of sound and music; and I think that thought is true. "Before all things, Sound."

She, the creatrix, means him to become himself a creator, a maker, to evoke order out of disorder, concord out of things discordant, to form and reform, may be to become the grand reformer of all time, destined to lead the world back to her. See him already in the cradle or seated on the floor arranging, rearranging coloured balls of worsted, making of them lines, crosses, square circles and odder conformations according to his own private aesthetic conceptions. Then he, replacing all carefully in their receptacle, enjoys a brief sabbath of rest and quiet self-satisfaction; but soon begins again, de novo, giving trouble to no one, absorbed, rapt in himself and his divine play, divine because creative, as, doubtless all play was meant by Nature to be. I believe that all Labour, that is all creative activity was meant by her to be, mainly, Play, and all Play, too, to be, in the main, creative activity, that is, Labour. Who has sensualised, degraded the divine creative activity, Labour, made it forced and servile, and filled it with want and suffering and self-contempt? Not the divine Mother, surely. See her beautiful ways with this child of hers while as yet no hostile power has thrust itself between these lovers, between her and him, between Nature and Man.

She bids him move, propel himself, exert his bodily powers, bring forth the concealed strength which she has stored in his limbs and his still soft and gristly little bones. See him, the active little quadruped, who is no quadruped though four-footed, see him crawling, then racing, and every day faster and ever faster across the floor, watched always by his loving Mother, the earthly one, as she sits and sews. Madonna! Is it a wonder that men should have worshipped you? Mother of God! Perhaps.

He is a healthy little hero and a happy; happiness coming with health and health with happiness. From his little pure person and glossy gold hair is exhaled a fragrance as of flowers.

And now the great moment has arrived when the unseen Mother bids him be a Man, not a little quadruped; commands him to stand upright on his feet. Because she has:—

> *Os homini sublime dedit caelumque tueri*
> *Jussit et erectos ad sidera tollere vultus.*[3]

as sang beautiful Vergil long ago in his rolling hexameters.

And our hero, like a little soldier, obeys the word of command. He stands upright on dispread feet and astonishes the household: a great event. Father, returning home, is greeted with the glad news.

According to a beautiful peasant Irish hymn, the first joy of the Blessed Virgin was hers when her dear Son, our Lord, got that degree of strength that he was able to be born. Her second joy was when he got sufficient strength to be able to stand on his feet and walk upon the floor! Have we not here a beautiful commingling of Nature worship and Christianity?

She sends him into her beautiful sunlight and he goes; bids him notice the grass, the flowers, the visiting bees, the sturdy strong-trunked trees, the stream singing as it runs, the birds, the black cawing rook, the gliding swallow, the strange attractive animals so like himself, so unlike. She bids him feel the interest, be aware of the fascination, and he obeys.

She means him, later, to command, therefore bids him first serve, and he serves, gladly, proudly, rejoices to be sent on messages, to carry things, to be a help. It is a great day when he is first permitted to ride the cart-horse to water. The big cart-horse stoops to drink; his shoulders collapse astonishingly and our hero slides down along his neck into the river. Our little hero, you see, is country-bred, as every little one ought to be, and has come out upon the world from a well-conditioned home, such a home as Nature loves.

She bids him learn more and more about her beautiful external world: bids him explore; and he goes exploring. He wanders delighted up and down that fascinating stream: wonders at the silent trout there so very thirsty, drinking, always drinking, captures pinkeens, finds that they can stab him, wonders at the falls and the rapids and the quiet pools. He falls in love with all—with the sword-shaped beautiful water-flags, the rushes, the graceful tall reeds, the little groves of manly bulrushes. A king-fisher darts past in his splendour and beauty: a water-ouzel scurries over the rapids, twisting cleverly between foaming boulders. Once he sees him near at hand, walking at the bottom! Marvellous! The water-hen sails from bank to bank; the vole swims across the pool, making a long V upon the still water with his little painted nose.

One day he has an odd experience: There is a secluded deep still pool, girt by honeysuckle, blossomed thorn, wild roses, golden furze, and a sense comes upon him of people there surprised, indignant, at his rude intrusion. A little Greek would understand why he felt so, being a Christian, a latter-day one, he does not.

He follows the stream up and up; finds its source in a little mossy well under an ancient twisted thorn. This is very satisfactory, very. He sits by the well and looks down and around; did not know that the world was so big, or his own house lawn and familiar fields so small.

THREE.

CHILD, TEACHER AND BOOK[4]

FOUR.

CHILDREN AND ANIMALS.

A friendly critic denies strenuously my assertion that boys are naturally lovers of birds and beasts, and reasserts the popular notion that in this respect they are naturally cruel.

It is very important how we decide this question. It will make an enormous practical difference in our methods of education whether we have to deal with a powerful current of boyish emotion setting towards an affectionate interest in birds and beasts, or with one which sets towards their pursuit and destruction, whether in the boy, as he is by nature, we have a lover of these wild existences, or a little two-legged fiend to be strongly over-controlled and checked and thwarted, and taught such kindness contrary to strong natural inclination.

Now, boys are proverbially fond of pets and very readily and gladly contract friendships with living creatures, even with reptiles! even enjoy keeping insects and studying their ways. This is a very remarkable fact, and shows the young mind fresh from Nature's creative hands, inspired by a very wide and quite spontaneous sympathy with living things. Give the boy that freedom and leisure to which he is entitled, spending his early years in the country with liberty of access to woods fields and waters, and this great interest seems to start up quite of its own accord. The educator need only be at hand to help and direct: Nature supplies the rest. The boy very readily and joyfully appropriates some or many of the wild existences, takes care of them, and observes them. This is a fact, not a theory.

As to animals already domesticated, his natural feelings are certainly friendly and kindly, not cruel, though it is in the wild creatures whom he is himself trying to domesticate that he takes the greatest interest.

Let me tell a story of my own boyhood: One morning—I was about six at the time—I learned that a sheep was about to be killed, and that the deed was to be done in one of the outhouses in the stable in fact. I determined to witness the event though my father had given strict orders against any of us being present on such an occasion.

I knew by experience that there were some things so forbidden which were distinctly good, *mala prohibita*, indeed, but indubitably *bona in se*. The chief of these forbidden things was the breaking of the Sabbath by climbing trees, jumping, running races, etc., for an extreme Puritanism reigned in our home. I concluded without doubt that the deed to be done in the stable was a joy, the prohibition establishing the fact. I believe that against commands which they do not understand, against prohibitions which represent only an external authority, boys are by nature rebellious, and I am glad of the fact. The boy is already a rational being and should be treated as such. The much-revolving child-mind demands, though dumbly, to be brought into the council-chamber.

Lest old Curly, the butcher on this occasion, should exclude me from the place of execution I secreted myself in the room overhead amid the hay, and there waited till the great forbidden joy should be in progress below. Judging from certain heard noises that the time had come, I climbed down by the bars of the hay rack, and saw the whole abomination.

For the first time in my life, and, never since in anything like the same degree, I experienced the sense of horror. I go further. I say that the horror was more than human and natural, that there was in it something preternatural. The whole world seemed to grow black and tremble. I saw, or seemed to see, the sun red in a black sky. You may say that I have since then imagined such an experience, though I don't believe it. I have a very vivid and distinct memory of what then happened—the nameless horror, and the blackness, the shaking world and the red sun. At all events something then happened, sudden, terrible, and appalling. I have never told this story in my life, nor would now but that I have a most serious purpose to subserve. I hope to convince parents guardians and teachers that the boy is, by nature, a lover of animals. I never had a lamb pet as a boy, and took no particular interest at all in sheep; knew them only as woolly things roaming about the place, causing much annoyance, too, by getting over fences and eating forbidden food; and now and then getting thrown down and shorn. Then, in that slaughter scene, I had expected to witness some interesting and delightful event; some rare kind of delight that grown-up people wished to keep to themselves. Yet this supernatural terror and horror was what I experienced. Lately I read in the much-maligned works of the French economist, Fourier,[5] that in the reign of "Harmony"—Fourier's name for the ideal social state—boys and girls would constitute the courts for the trial of persons charged with cruelty to animals. There is always something worth thinking of even in Fourier's most flagrant paradoxes. Boys, as the greatest animal-lovers of us all, will be, I venture to predict, the natural protectors of all dumb creatures and the chief guardians of their rights. But the boys have not had fair play. Millions of them get no chance at all of making friends with animals, of having and keeping pets. Give any little boy a donkey only, and you will see. Let me tell you another story.

I was once cycling in the County Dublin and met a little boy riding his ass to town. I stopped him and asked him would he sell me the donkey. He sprang to the ground, and, putting one arm round his donkey's neck, looked at me with laughing saucy eyes.

"How much would you give me for him?"

"Perhaps Two Pounds," I said.

" Wouldn't you give me any more than that?"

"Well, I might go as far as £2. 10s. 0d. if I like him after trial."

"Would you now?" said he, looking more and more saucy. Then suddenly, looking grave and defiant: "I wouldn't sell him to you, not if you gave me the whole world for him."

So saying he sprang on his donkey's back and was out of sight in a moment.

There spoke the true boy, the genuine boy, such as most boys would be if we only gave them fair play, were we to bring them up in the country, gave them leisure and freedom and allowed their beautiful instincts loves and passions, to grow as Nature meant that they should. And is it not a shame, seeing that boys are like that, that we bring them up by millions in conditions under which they can never make such friends at all, and then expect them to grow up kind and good? In the education of boys pets are far more important than pedagogues.

The natural man is seen best in the child, for as he grows up he gradually assumes a second nature impressed upon him by the social world that surrounds him. The real mind of man is discovered also in literature and in literature this natural friendship of man and the animals is a pronounced and universal feature.

In Paradise, Adam, that is Man, did not chase and slay the animals. They came to him, in friendly wise, to be named. I know that the whole story is only a legend, but in this, as in nearly all the legends, there is something at the same time touchingly childlike and profoundly true. If men never knew children, if they did not remember their own child-life, [they] never would have created for themselves such legends. Our Bible Paradise story came out of the child-mind.

The Greek and Italian classical nations believed in an "Age of Gold". They believed that a strict amity then prevailed between men and the animals—what Burns calls "Nature's social union"—that men did not hurt the animals and that the animals did not hurt men. The mention of Burns reminds me that the Poets, who are more like children than the rest of us, have been nearly all or quite all of them on the side of the animals: very tender, gentle and considerate to the animals as they are to all weak things, to children and the backward savage races, and to old people and to women. I am thinking just now of our modern Poets. I recall them and with great joy: Cowper, Burns, Goldsmith, Scott, Byron, Wordsworth, Whitman. The finest celebration, so far, of the animals comes from Walt Whitman: "They are so placid and so self-contained", etc.[6]

I think it is a reasonable argument. We cannot get at the child-mind in its natural state; but that mind may be, I believe, best discovered in the Poets who, in so many other respects, bear a near resemblance to children.

The child's mind is captured and corrupted before it can exhibit its true nature. Our little petticoated Prophet is corrupted and perverted by the Mature before he can begin to prophesy. Wordsworth, remember, names the child—a Prophet, and even a "mighty Prophet".[7] And he was right.

As primitive man moved on towards Civilisation, the Child was his leader. This was seen by the great Roman poet, Lucretius, who, too, I may say in passing, loved the animals well. He and Ovid have written their noblest, most divinely inspired verses about the animals.

The water-wag-tail stands on a stone in the river, his long tail ceaselessly oscillating. The man walks by, his thoughts bent upon higher things. The boys pauses, observes, carefully chooses a stone and shies it at the little bird. Splash! And water-wag-tail is off; escapes to securer regions.

The man thinks the boy a cruel, mischievous little brat, [and he] if in the humour may deliver himself of a stupid homily. But the boy was interested in the little bird; the man was not.

Just as the unborn child repeats swiftly those countless phases of existence through which Man has passed in his cyclic evolution, so when born and while he still goes on all fours, he is as certainly repeating the life of a pre-human progenitor. The child of ten months is unable to stand upright and walk on two feet, not from want of strength but because his bodily conformation is still that of a pre-human ancestor. So we may be certain that in his playfulness, happiness, smiles, laughter, affectionateness, simplicity, innocence and docility, he is repeating characteristics of an early human ancestry.

Primitive man emerging from his native forests was like that. He came out of the woods laughing. I cannot at all accept the notion of primitive man as a gloomy cave-dwelling savage issuing forth, armed with club and stone to fight desperately for his life with mastodon and sabre-tooth and other fierce creatures of the earth. How could such a being alternately killing and being killed ever have learned to smile, laugh, and be glad and gay like the child.

We are all in ignorance here, each with a right to his own thought. I believe that man first emerged upon the earth and into the society of animals resembling very much the child, and that he was protected against wild beasts, not by his ferocity and cunning, his deftly wielded club and well-thrown stone, but by his innocence and fearlessness, his strange upright attitude, and his smiling expressive inexplicable countenance. The animals wondered at him as at a god; Sabre-tooth reserved his fangs and claws for a different kind of prey.

Milton describes the animals in Paradise as sporting before the first man eager to attract his attention, and one of the Hebrew Poets imagines the lion and the leopard led by the Child. These are poetic dreams; but the dreams of such children of wisdom pierce far into the truth of things.

Recall another of those dreams: When the Holy Family crossed the desert on their journey into Egypt, a herd of lions marched in front and of leopards in the rear, wolves went on either side gambolling and barking joyously, and serpents stood up and out of their holes and made obeisance to the Divine Child as he passed.

Such dreams—and they are many—spring from a deep human intuition that Man, as to his essential nature, is innocent, beautiful and childlike and that he and the animals are naturally friends bound by nature in a league of amity which at some time and for some unknown reason Man broke, but which he will yet renew. The Poets and the children are leading the way. It was a true Poet who sang:—

> "A robin red-Breast in a cage
> Puts all Heaven in a rage." [8]

Also it is a fact that in all Ireland, and I daresay in all Great Britain there is not a child who would dare cage a redbreast.

Mankind will be led back to Paradise by the Children and the Poets.

If I did not myself believe in the return to Paradise, I mean of course the World-Paradise, and to that amity between ourselves, between man and man, and between men and all living things, I would never have taken the pains to write this book and set up such a misunderstanding between myself and others; as this book must unavoidably involve. For I am perfectly aware of the scoffing and jeering and perhaps even hatred which must follow.

However, if I err it is in good company. Burns, who addressed the field-mouse as his "earth-born companion"[9] and who lamented that his presence had scared the waterfowl of Lough Urit from their quiet home, wrote too:

> "For a' that, and a' that
> It's coming yet for a' that,
> That man with man, the world around,
> Shall brothers be, for a' that."[10]

However, now leaving these larger themes, I suggest to all parents and guardians that they should strain every means at their command to enable their children to indulge to the utmost their natural love of natural history. It is Nature's own way of educating at the same time both their minds and their hearts. If they wish even to keep serpents in your house I would almost say—"let them".

When I was a boy myself I lived in the very happiest surroundings, woods streams mountains and the sea, but lost a great deal through having no natural history books and no one to answer almost any of my questions.

See that your children have such books, well illustrated, and that there is some one at hand to tell them anything they want to know. Don't force the young mind in any direction. Nature is infinitely wiser than we are, and may be trusted to take the best care of all the children whom she sends into the world.

It will be asked:— "If primitive man was as you say child-like and innocent and friendly with the beasts of the field how did he ever come to wage war upon them, slay and eat them?" It is, I suppose, part of the mystery of the origin of evil, but I would suggest that through some convulsion of the Earth's surface, or some other cause, he found himself separated from these forests or fertile places which first supplied him with food and that he first slew and ate animals for the same reason that sometimes today compels men to descend to cannibalism. Once more I would ask whence, if not from a remote ancestry resembling themselves, did our children get those innocent, merry, smiling and laughing countenances of theirs, their fearlessness and their singular passionate interest in the living creatures which surround them?

If the opposing theory were true, children ought to begin by being dour fierce terrible, in the extreme, gradually growing in gentleness as they approach maturity. Yet it is not so.

FIVE.

A WELCOME VISITOR.

SHADOWS

The great friendship began in a paper chase in which our hero, youngest of the crew, was cruelly abandoned, left alone, all alone in the wide world. From the wrong side of a hideous black drain he lifted up his voice in a loud and bitter wail. One of the bigger boys, his heart touched by the appealing cry, ran back, called him "a little ninny", helped him over that deep and dark gulf and during the rest of the chase saw him safe over all obstructions. Result—love deep, and great, and lasting.

Sandy was the friend's name; a great draughtsman: marvellous at the portrayal of whales and whale hunting, whales quiescent or grandly spouting: valiant harpooners with weapon poised or hurled, the coiling rope uncoiling; boats tossed high in air by a flip of the mighty one's tail, and astonished sailors falling sea-ward, upside down, preceded by their hair, etc., etc. Tad is introduced so into this new marvellous world of art, begins to draw, with great joy, and even paint. I sent him a box of colours. But, unlike Sandy, he loved better to reproduce things he knew and was familiar with. Very soon Nature begins to show that she intends for each of her children an individual distinctive career; all his own; a great fact ignored by educationists. She means her children to go each their own beautiful way, not along the muddy trodden roads of the grown-ups.

Ruskin says that children should not be compelled to read or write but that they should be compelled to draw.[11] Not much compulsion is necessary.

Though tirelessly active our hero is very well pleased at times to do nothing but sit and think; for, unlike us, the Fallen, he can well afford it. He is still in the Paradise which Nature has made for us all. Still with him the quiet Past and the miraculous resplendent Future unite beautifully in the radiant Present, in the passing moment as it flees, the mysterious three-stranded ever-running cord of Time and Life.

Men's happiness is to forget. Therefore by the man of the world politics, sport, business, society, lively conversation, amours, drink, all manner of distractions and diversions are welcome: anything that holds his mind on the passing moment and excludes time past and time coming. He endeavours, so, to grasp the felicity of the beast; and can't; just because Nature made him a man not a beast. "*Carpe diem*" sang old Horace while he himself could never forget the *anni fugaces* and *Libitina*[12] coming on with great strides. We know the advice to be good, but can't practise it. Our hero practises it without knowing anything of the good advice. The bewildered Christian hears and reads the command of his Master "Take no thought for the morrow", while the morrow is writing lines of care all over his pious countenance.

When men begin to live again as Nature intended them to live they will resemble the child in many ways and especially in this. They will live in the present—looking with hope and confidence upon the future.

"But the world will not permit us to live so."

Yes, I know that. But what follows? This, that if men would live as their Maker and Sustainer meant them to live, and as the child does, they must get outside of this mighty reticulation of laws, rules, customs and habits which we call the World. You can't reform the World; it is too strong for you. Live within its empire and it will inevitably conquer you and make you one with itself. To be free you must be outside its dominion. This I believe is the truth which underlies that strange utterance, "You must be born again."[13]

Later we may consider that. Meantime note that, within the World, as the shadows begin to close around the child, the glowing radiant moment is for him dashed and darkened by the Future. Sinister alarms and apprehensions emanating from the future begin to throng around him. Even our quite young people have to forget that future in order to be gay. Have they not to "get on", if they would not be trampled on and perish? While the great terror of not getting on impends above them.

Nature gives to all her other creatures the Present only. In action or at rest the passing moment only is theirs: but Nature for them makes the passing moment sweet and glad. To Man alone she has given the two great other worlds with remembrance and hope and imagination. But having rebelled against her and separated himself from her he cannot possess those worlds. If he thinks, that is ventures into them, he is unhappy, the Past holds such misfortunes and the Future is so filled with fear. Therefore it is his sorry wisdom to get all he can out of the Present: his happiness is to forget. Such is the absurd world that he has made for himself.

"Where but to think is to be full of sorrow."[14] A sentiment expressed by many of our poets, though I remember that the gallant Bobbie Burns enumerating the pleasures of his life records gratefully:—

"I ha'e been happy thinking".[15] For poets, indeed all men of original genius, do often contrive to carry with them into maturity a good deal of the child-life.

And indeed there is no better bit of worldly wisdom than this:— "Live, all you can, in the Present. *Carpe diem.* Let life be a continual nowness."

It is not divine wisdom but is good worldly wisdom; though exceedingly hard for us worldly folk to practise.

Meantime she who made us and sustains us, holy Nature, the infinitely wise and good, is saying to us continually:— "Live with me and I will give you all that the little child has and far more."

When I first met our hero he was just six. At the house they told me I should find him "in the wood". Crossing the lawn I presently heard an animated whistling and vigorous drumming which came out of the depths of the wood, and soon beheld the little man himself marching smartly between the trees drumming vigorously with one hand and holding a whistle to his mouth with the other, and so absorbed in that martial occupation that he came quite near without noticing me. He turned round smartly and marched back showing me a noble pair of little brown calves as he went and twisting cleverly round and in and out between the trees.

On his return I stepped forward to meet him. He stood still a moment contemplating me with large eyes not the least shy or alarmed and coming forward put his hand in mine. I had a great mind to take him up and kiss him on the spot, but thought he was a little too big for such treatment and might not like it.

"You're Tad," I said.

"I am."

"Well, I'm a friend of your father's—I'm to have supper with you to-night."

"That will be nice. There will be jam and honey and strawberries."

I was overjoyed.

"Would you like to see my robin's nest?" he said.

"Very much."

He led me through the wood which was rarely carpeted with pine-needles up a rocky ascent, and, with a warning look and gesture, brought me to the foot of that pine tree, parted the primrose leaves with his little drumstick and bade me look. There indeed she was, the robin, brooding on her eggs, her little eyes shining bright as diamonds in the dusk, and quite unalarmed.

"She does not like everyone," observed Tad, as he drew me away. "Yesterday when Mr. Dunscombe was looking in at her she got frightened at his face and fled away: or perhaps it was his black clothes that frightened her. You did not frighten her at all."

"I'm very glad; it was a great compliment. And I know what Mr Dunscombe did when the robin flew away. He stood up straight with his hands clasped before him and shook his head slowly up and down, like this. Then he said something just as if he was reading out of a book."

Tad's laugh rang out merrily at my sorrowful head-nodding in imitation of the very learned clergyman of that parish.

"Yes: he did," cried Tad. And he said a verse of a hymn. There was— "I'm truly sorry in the hymn; but he said, 'I'm truly sorry,' three or four times shaking his head up and down just like you did."

"Do you remember anything else in the hymn except 'I'm truly sorry'?"

"Yes. There was 'Man's dominion' in it too; I remember that: 'Man's dominion.'"

"I know the hymn now," I said.

"I'm truly sorry Man's dominion
   Has broken Nature's social union
And justifies the ill opinion
   That makes thee startle
At me thy poor earth-born companion and fellow mortal."[16]

"That was it," cried Tad. "That was the hymn."

I told him the story of Burns and the mouse. How, with winter coming on, Burns had ploughed up mousie's house, and how sorry he was, because winter was coming on.

"I know that kind of mouse," said Tad. "He's smaller than the indoors mouse. They're very clever little chaps. Do you think he was able to make a new house before the frost came and hardened the ground?"

"I'm sure of it."

"Was Burns a clergyman?"

"Well, yes: I think he was: but unordained. He did not wear a white tie or black clothes."

Seeing a sycamore tree hard by I proposed to make a whistle out of one of the branches, which I did, by drawing off the peel and hollowing out the timber. Then replacing the peel I presented him with the finished whistle, which he blew joyously. Next he would make one of his own, which he did, successfully; save that he was not strong enough to twist off the peel. I rose greatly in Tad's estimation by making that whistle.

"You must be very careful about penknives, Tad" I said. "When I was a little boy like you I was not; and cut myself badly." I showed him my left hand full of ancient scars, lasting mementoes of youthful impetuosity.

Then I produced out of its wrapper a present which I had brought him from Town. It was a bow and arrows, and we spent the rest of the afternoon shooting arrows at the stem of a little holly tree which grew on the lawn. He was not a beautiful child but winning in his ways, brimful of health and vitality, his face brown from the sun and wind and freckled all over like a turkey's egg. He was just one of the millions of children whom Nature is continually sending into the world but one of the very few who get a little fair play at the start.

For supper he had a big mug of milk and a plate of brown bread and butter which he finished off in fine style, in silence. Later on, when he was in bed, solid Joseph, guardian and trustee, talked with me about stocks and shares. He had some funds to invest for "Mary and the lad," and was rather drawn towards "Japanese securities." While he slowly talked and pondered and thoughtfully ran his fingers through his huge beard, the large dark prophet eyes of Madonna were uplifted more and more as her spirit continued commercing with I know not what celestial things.

"When he grows up, Mrs Egerton," said I, "what would you like him best to be?"

"A soldier," said Madonna, lowering her eyes and letting her overpowering glance rest gently on me.

"A soldier!" I cried.

"Yes."[17]

PART II.

NATURE AND MAN.

NATURA NATURANS.

ONE.

NATURE.

The word Nature, beautiful in itself, is more beautiful to one who knows its Latin origin, *Natura*. Observe the delicate future signification, remembering "The Future in Rus"[18] of our schoolboy days. *Natura*, in its full form, *Res Natura*, means the Being who is always about to be born, always becoming, manifesting. I think when the phrase was first invented, and surely it was by a great poet, *Natura* had in his mind an active signification more than a passive; and meant the Being who is continually bringing to Birth; and so the Mother. Also, Matter, *Materies*, means the Mother—Substance. If you take these words together, Matter and Nature, remembering their root-meanings, you will see how deeply the feeling of the Maternity of being held the minds of the ancient poets and philosophers of the great Italian race to whom we owe these words, and so much else. What those unknown ancient Italian thinkers were like we can partly guess from the writings of Vergil and Lucretius.

All the ancient peoples, wise and simple, felt that Nature was their Mother, they her children, and expressed that deep feeling in a thousand different ways, in their languages, philosophies, mythologies, religious practices, and daily thoughts and habits. The Greek gentleman leaving his house in the morning tapped the earth with foot or staff and said: "Chairee, O Gaia" "Hail, O Earth", or as we might say, "God bless thee, good Earth!" The Greek doctor, as he went forth in the morning to cull simples in the woods and fields, carried his digging tool in the right hand and a pitcher in the left. It contained a mixture of milk, wine, flour, and honey. According as he unearthed any medicinal plant he murmured a prayer of praise and thanksgiving, and a petition for pardon to the good Earth for the unsightly gash which he had made in her sacred bosom. Then out of his pitcher he poured a peace offering into the wound. The Italian was much the same; and so we can understand how that which is so dead and dull with us, so common, vulgar and prosaic, the Earth, humus, mould, "mere matter", was to him *Materies*, Mother-Substance, the visible form and very body of the Creatress, the divine Mother of all things. The very Earth he walked upon was divine.

Most of us even today, I think, have a feeling like this, though a little shy of expressing it. We all at our best moments revere and love the Earth well:

"The tread of my foot on the Earth starts a thousand affections."

That universal and absolutely right and natural feeling of our Aryan ancestors has been obscured in more modern Europe by the prevalence of Semitic fanaticisms, the devotion to divers gods and demons made in the likeness of corrupt mankind; but it has been here always nevertheless; and always will be. The love of Nature, the all-Mother, has ever lain deep in the European heart and in modern times has found noble expression through our great Nature poets, the English poets leading in that respect: Wordsworth, Shelley, Scott, Byron, and Keats. In this context re-read Shelley's Hymn to Asia in the "Prometheus Unbound". In this impassioned lyric Asia is Nature, Heaven and Earth and the spirit which animates them conceived and felt towards as if feminine.

Though no poet I, too, in plain prose would add my tribute of love and praise and gratitude to her in whose womb I was fashioned and to whom, in her own good time, I return, like everything created.

Nature is for ever and everywhere producing such multitudes of beautiful things that even where we do not see her to be beautiful we know that she is, that she is beautiful through and through and everywhere and for ever. Our faith in that respect is not in the least affected by her seeming unlovelinesses, her noxious creatures, weeds, desert wastes, the unwelcome mysteries of decay and death. We know they are there, know, too, that we don't understand, that we are not permitted to understand: for reasons.

We know that, these unlovelinesses notwithstanding, Nature is beautiful through and through, that she is one with Beauty; is Beauty; and that Beauty made the world. Made it! Nay, makes it from moment to moment and lives and reigns through all its vastnesses and incomprehensibilities. Not only is the world beautiful, it is infinitely beautiful. We cannot imagine it more so: nor think of any way in which it can be made more beautiful.

Perfect is a weak word but it must serve here. Nature is perfect. We are surrounded on all sides by the perfection of Beauty. And this sovereign Beauty, which is Nature, has created Man, too, Man as well as the revolving universes, as well as the grass, flowers, trees, rivers, mountains, birds and beasts, fishes and insects. She has raised him up on high, out far beyond all his natural kindred. She has endowed him with intellect, imagination, hope and memory, flowing love, quick compassion and tenderness, and a godlike pride, erecting his form and setting his face to far horizons, to Heaven and the Stars. She has given him the lordship of the Planet and made him a visible god to all her other creatures, so far as they have perception and intelligence, removing him far from their plane and outside their comprehension. He is her chief work and the crown of her creation. The sovereign Beauty which is Nature, made him too, yet he is un-beautiful, even to himself. Here, and here only, we are compelled to believe that she has been baulked and frustrated. Why? Why is Man the only un-lovely thing in her world-paradise, un-beautiful though erect and with his face to far horizons, to Heaven and the Stars? Un-beautiful in spite of his marvellous equipment and though he is Nature's chief work and the crown of all her creation?

Again, the World-Paradise which is Beauty to the eye is Music to the ear. Nature has, for her own deep reasons, dulled in us, temporarily, the divine sense of hearing. But we hear enough and know enough to be aware that we live in the midst of an infinite ocean of Music. All things are in motion, vibration; therefore full of sound, therefore full of Music. We don't hear the harmonies but know they are there. All the poets from before and since Plato have been deeply aware of it. The originators of religions, the makers of myths have known it; the thought underlies their words and institutions. In our own Gaelic mythology do not the seasons in beautiful procession come forth and pass to the music of the Dagda's pipe as he plays? Before Light itself did not the Semitic vales set sound.

And God said, "Let there be Light."

While another made the singing of the starry host contemporaneous with the act of creation:

"From harmony from heavenly harmony
This universal frame began."[19]

If Nature is Beauty, as she is, so, too, she is Music. But in the midst of all the Music there is one harsh discord. Man is that. We are the one discordant and terribly dissonant note in the great harmony. Nature here too has been defeated, baulked, frustrated. Why?

Once more, the world has been made by Wisdom as by Music and Beauty. We cannot study any one single thing without being aware that an infinite Wisdom is present in its creation, preservation, even in its disintegration. In some ways this profound Wisdom resembles our poor human intelligence, suggests our limited provision of ways and means to accomplish ends, but it is infinitely more than this. An intelligent child can understand the construction of the greatest of our works. The savants of all the Earth can only stare helplessly after the little thistle-down as it floats in Autumn down the breeze. Neither the thistle nor its winged seed can they understand; no, nor a single atom or fibre in the miraculous structure of the little aeronaut. If the poor savant is any good, he knows that he knows nothing. And this an unfathomable Wisdom with deep below deep, height beyond height, has made and is reflected by everything created except Man. Why? Why is Man so silly, insane, in the midst of universal Wisdom, having been created by that Wisdom.

Once more, everything that Nature creates is happy, glad, and gay, rejoicing, exulting in its life, each according to its kind and degree. Nature, which is Wisdom and Music and Beauty, is also Joy, happiness, contentment, delight and exultation. Nature exulting and delighted, made us too. Yet in the midst of the rejoicing World, Man alone walks the Earth unhappy— a wretch! The only one of Nature's creatures which slays itself on account of its unendurable misery. Why?

In the midst of infinite Beauty he is un-lovely: of infinite Harmony, a discord. Of infinite Wisdom, a Madman. In the midst of Joy he is unhappy, the one unhappy thing in the wide world. Shelley, who never thinks of Nature save as one with Wisdom, Music, and Beauty, treats her, too, as one with Delight, with the pure "Spirit of Delight," in lines so lovely that I am compelled to repeat them:

> "I love all that thou lovest,
> Spirit of Delight.
> The fresh Earth in new leaves drest,
> And the blessed night,
> Starry evening and the morn
> When the golden mists are born.
>
> I love snow and all the forms
> Of the radiant frost,
> I love winds and waves and storms,
> Everything almost
> That is Nature's and may be
> Untainted by Man's misery."[20]

Again, all Nature's creatures enjoy the infinite blessing, the beatitude of Health. Like Beauty, like Music, like Joy, for which it is only another name, Health, too, rushes out over all the world in infinite streams; Health which is also Sanity, also Balance. Man only is diseased. He is the one sick thing on the face of the Earth. Why? Nature made Man, too; made him with infinite care, equipped him marvellously for the marvellous road that she meant him to travel. Why is he such a wretched sick thing, losing his teeth in his teens, afflicted with more diseases than the wonderfully compliant Greek tongue can supply names for? We know that Nature made him, and from a speck, an atom, a mere nothing; guided him upwards, through countless grades of being, is doing so again today in the darkness of his Mother's womb, and gave him intelligence and foresight and imagination and love, and equipped him in millions of subtle ways to be worthy of her, to resemble her, to reflect, a little, her infinite perfection. Yet he comes up diseased, the only sick animal on the Planet. Why?

Then, Nature, in spite of her occasional and momentary beneficent storms and convulsions, is very quiet, gentle and serene, peace-loving and peace-breathing, peace-diffusing. Perturbed, excited, self-tormented to and almost over the line that divides him from sheer insanity, Man, sometimes, comes face to face with her quiet spirit, with her motion that seems to be rest, and her rest which is in motion, comes face to face with her and is astonished; oft-times, too, healed and soothed by that blessed contact, as the crying child is sweetly aware of the caressing hands and gentle low persuading voice of its Mother. He has a familiar proverb which declares that "it is vulgar to be in a hurry". If she were, she would slay us all, like those angry vulgar man-resembling gods of old time. But she is not, not in a hurry; never was, or is, or will be. She knows that having caused all other things to yield to her gentle sway she will, in the end, cause Man, too, to return to her with a very repentant, sincere *peccavi*; and in the meantime she waits full of love and tenderness, knowing that she must not and cannot force us to return to her, that we must return to her of our own free will. For she made us like that, able to leave her but also able to return.

"Loving too! I suppose that you will be next saying that Nature and Love are one, and that Love made all things!"

Yes, assuredly. Nature is Love, too. Love made all things. Love made Man, too, so filled, as he is, with fear and hatred as to be ever at the murder-point, ever revolving thoughts of self-destruction or of the destruction of others. We know that it needs but a touch today to let loose murderous agencies which will desolate half the globe. Yet this hater and murderer was begotten and conceived in Love, and is so today. Every murderer on the face of the Earth and all the good men and the gentle women who, out of the security of their social fast-nesses, train and equip the murderers and send them forth and applaud them, who maintain these be-bannered hosts by land and sea, drilled to perfection, tremendously weaponed, gorgeously caparisoned—all and each were begotten and conceived in Love, love rudely casual or true tender and faithful, and whether Pandemic or Uranian, yet in Love, in the Love of Man and Woman, earthly shadow of the Love which made and makes the world, the Love of Nature and her Lord, of the Spirit and the Bride.

"You begin to speak in riddles. What do you mean by the Spirit and the Bride?"

I cannot explain at present, hardly even at all, but at leisure read carefully the last chapter of our own sacred Scripture and draw your own inference. Under that strange Jewish symbology you will find hidden certain eternal truths.

"I have passed over in silence the rest of your dithyrhambics, your ascription to Nature of all that is best in Man and that raised to the height of infinity; but when you say she is Love, too, I rebel."

I take it that you are at least not unwilling to accept provisionally at least and as a subject for meditation all the rest of my poor prosaic praise and lame laudations of the great Mother. I say now that she is Love, too; Love as well as Health and Gladness, and Wisdom, and Music, and Beauty. Listen!

I once met a woman who was indescribably beautiful. Her voice was Music, her every movement a harmony. Youth, health, vitality, mantled rose-red in her cheeks and lips, shone in her glowing and flashing eyes, her perfect form, her light elastic step and beautiful gestures. She was wise, too, beyond all other women, but such was her gentleness and graciousness, such her humility that she veiled her wisdom. She was intensely, rapturously happy, and diffused an atmosphere of joy all round her and at every moment and by night as by day. But she had one defect.

"One defect! It is impossible; for you are describing perfection."

She loved nothing, nor anyone. Wonderfully, miraculously gifted otherwise, she had no heart or soul.

"It is incredible."

You are right. It is; it is incredible. Therefore, Nature being in all other respects the infinity of perfection must be Love too. Love made, created, and for ever recreates the world. Nature, who is Love, made us too in her own image. Why are we so unloving?

"Yes, that is a puzzle. We ought at least not to hurt and prey upon each other whether the power that made us be what you hold it to be or not. But you seem to be using the language of fancy and imagination, not that of the sober and exact thinker, in all these holdings forth of yours about Nature, her goodness and beauty. *Natura* is, no doubt, a feminine word, and so lends itself seductively to the pleasing illusion that the thing indicated is feminine too. You seem to mistake your metaphors and symbols for realities."

I think not, not quite. For, consider, it seems to be a necessity of human thought, this use of symbols, signs, and metaphors. All words are symbols. Symbol (the casting together of things) is itself a symbol, a mere sign, and the component parts of the word[21] were both metaphors in the mind and in the mouths of the ancient Greeks who first used them.

Necessity, some deep insuperable law of the human mind, compels us to use symbols, to employ visible things, things readily apprehensible to express the invisible and incomprehensible. There is a very intimate and vital relation between the accepted symbol and the thing symbolised. The flag of a crack regiment, the little bit of emblazoned wool and cotton for whose sake a thousand brave men will permit themselves to be slashed into horrid death; the upright log, which was at the same time the banner and the god and natural emblem of the primitive Greek clan; the ark of the Israelite nation, are signs, if you will; but there has incorporated itself in them something divine, unearthly, eternal, something quite as real as, nay, infinitely more real, than the visible symbol—poor transitory fragile thing, here today gone tomorrow.

Nature, *Natura*, conceived and felt towards as feminine, as the divine mother of mankind and all things, creatrix and nutrix, is doubtless a symbol, but one to which the mind of man is compelled by a certain necessity. In thought, feeling, and expression I but follow great precedents. Great poets, prophets, and seers, philosophers, and what is still more and far more charged with meaning—the coming and passing multitudes of mankind with their instinctive wisdoms, their heart-cravings and aspirations, their humble pieties, enduring hope and trust and faith, have felt that the soul of the world is feminine, maternal, that a love like woman's, lies for ever in the heart of things.

Far away back in the depths of time we find this love of Nature permeating, often suffusing the impurer religions of infant mankind; sometimes it has even stood alone as the sole faith and dependence of man. Professor Ramsay[22] wandering, an explorer, through Asia Minor, stands astonished as the conviction is borne in upon him there that for countless ages the countless millions upon the vast Anatolian plains lived and died in this faith—the love of Nature, the all-Mother, and in this faith executed in friendly concert, and as if under her approving smile, the prodigious engineering works whose remains he beheld there.

So impressed was Professor Ramsay that he has published his belief in "The Age of Gold" of the classic poets, that it was no fable, that there actually was a time when men did not slay or wrong each other, but lived side by side in fraternal,

mutually assistful and co-operative societies, having for their
sole religion this love, trust, and faith in holy Nature. They
loved Nature and they prospered greatly.

" . . . For Nature never did betray
The heart that trusted her."[23]

Again, recent excavations in Crete have revealed there the
presence in a far distant time of a great and pre-Hellenic
Cretan civilisation which commenced in the stone age. It has
been discovered that the Cretans, even while they still used
flint knives and axes and flint digging tools, made and sailed
beautiful ships, and portrayed them beautifully on exquisitely
shaped pottery, and were skilled in architecture, horticulture,
the care of animals, and other beautiful and humane arts, and
that this civilisation, so starting, rose, culminated, and declined
like a vast arch spanning millenniums of time. Note now,
that this civilisation rejected idols and images and temples and
all dark and fearsome superstitions and maintained itself solely
upon the love of Nature. The Cretans worshipped as Mother
the same eternal *ever-young* source of life, beauty and gladness,
to whose service our noble English poet, Wordsworth, and
while still a mere boy, resolved to consecrate his life and be
her poet, priest, and prophet. In that strong and pure faith
they flourished, not for hundreds of years but for thousands!
lived and died in this love of Nature and trust in her. Nor till
the on-coming of the invasive Hellenes with their manlike
gods and carved images, would they permit any symbol of her
to be set up in their midst more distinctive than the simple
Cretan shield or the two-headed Cretan axe. Here is something revealed out of the depths of time calculated to make
men think. For, lo! today for us, as then for those vanished
millions of Mediterranean peoples, the East reddens and the
golden sun leaps forth, the serene heavens are a stainless blue
or traversed by the wandering clouds and at night glitter
with innumerable stars; the sparkling waters laugh and run;
the mountains rise; the sliding snow falls; the winds blow loud
or low, and as they blow feed the springs of life and joy and
hope in man and bird and beast and every living thing. All

the mad religions have passed on or are passing, but the Mother,—ever-young, ever beautiful, has not passed, has not lost a whit of her primeval power and beauty. She is still the same as when infant mankind, leaving behind him all his four-footed kindred, stood erect and looked around and up with a wide-eyed wonder; and still, to us as to them, she whispers for ever into quiet listening souls:—

"Love me, trust me. Be what I wish you to be; do what I tell you to do. Come back to me and be happy. Why have you left me only to be mad and miserable? Come back; be what I wish you to be; do what I tell you to do. I love you."

That Cretan civilisation rooted in the love of Nature endured for more thousands of years than I like to say just at present, and surely Nature did not betray those hearts that trusted her, not till those hearts began to waver and wander and forget. Then came Pasiphae and Daedalus and the Minotaur, and the end. Observe, too, that whatever be our religion the love of Nature will always sweetly and beautifully accord with it, illuminating its darknesses, mitigating its ferocities, tranquillising its unrest. So it has ever been. All the superstitions from the beginning of Time have become less superstitious, less ferocious when their thralls felt descend upon them the cooling calming influence of Nature. In the age of *autos da fé* Saint Francis of Assisi called the good fire his brother and the snow his beautiful sister, and thought of the animals and birds [as] one family with himself. Can we imagine that pious youth, so gentle and brave, present and assisting while men in that good "brother the fire" roasted to death their own human brothers and sisters?[24] No. Whatever be your religion, and whatever God be the object of your devotions, only love Nature, too, and you cannot go so far wrong. The love of Nature will blend well with every kind of religion.

Of the many hymns which as a little boy I was made to learn by heart almost the only ones which I have remembered all my life with pleasure, have been those which give expression to natural piety. For example:—

"God made the Sun that shines so bright,
   He made the grass so green;
He made the flowers that smell so sweet
   In pretty colours seen.

God made the cow that gives nice milk,
   The horse for me to use.
I'll treat them kindly for His sake
   And ne'er His gifts abuse."

I should like Mothers to teach religion to their children always through some such mediums and as they do so to remember that such verses can mean little or nothing to the millions of children brought up in the mighty centres of civilisation.

Remember also that the real religion of the men in whom are embodied today the great driving forces of our world—their religion stripped of its hypocrisies and pretences is in fact—Money. Indeed every one of us is, necessarily, more or less held, dominated by this wild faith. And for the fury and fanaticism engendered by such a cult is there, can there be any such mitigation or assuagement than that which is yielded by loving vital contact with the primal sanities and beautiful tranquillity of Nature and her ways. Most of you who read this are grown up and with ways of life fixed, yet I would ask you to so use all your spare powers and material resources as to bring up in the country your children, or other people's children. And not only to bring them up there but to educate them there in the sunlight and pure air, and so to provide careers for them there that they will never feel even a momentary desire to aggravate the murderous congestion of the great congested centres. If you concentrate on this problem—a problem which is by no means intricate or complex—even a tithe of the mental powers and energy which you now spend upon your business, whatever it may be, you will quickly discover for yourself all the necessary ways and means. For Nature has made the natural life the way of least resistance, putting there a minimum of pain and a maximum of delight. We have passed far outside the dominion and authority of texts, yet I would ask you to think very seriously about one such:

"My yoke is easy."[25]

Nature too is saying that always, for ever; and it is true.

Why is Man such a blot on the fair face of Creation, who ought rather to resemble the Morning Star when he shines a resplendent splash of light in the just kindling Eastern sky. O Lucifer, Son of the Morning, how art thou fallen! Why is he such a blot and stain and monster and criminal on the face of the Earth, and ever has been, through all our lurid historic record, murderer, thief, liar, deceiver; so that History in the main, resembles a police calendar filled with crimes and insanities. A Roman once, in one day, crucified—not one man—but six thousand men along an Italian highway. From Rome to Cappua the gibbets with their quivering victims stood frequent as the telegraph poles upon our highways. And the flaying of men alive to make sport! And the *auto da fes* for the glory of Christ! And the wars—pious or for plunder. And are we less dead, brutal, impious, devilish? no, only stupider, more hard-hearted. Go through the great cities and observe and consider, listening for one brief moment to the explanations of the doctors, the wise men and prophets; only for one moment, for their gibberish is as if corpses were enabled to find horrible utterance, like nightmares explaining other nightmares in the midst of some huge evil dream.

How has man become such a monster, subter-bestial, subter-reptilian on the face of the Earth?

And there is another question which arises out of this:— "Why does he not anywhere ask himself that question?" He never asks the question; never fairly, sincerely, intelligently. Why? Mad—eager to learn all he can about atoms and ions, about the constitution of matter, how it stands related with the ether; all he can about a thousand things which are to him of little or no concernment; he utterly ignores this one question which is the necessary starting point of any serious enquiry concerning his own nature. More than that, he does his best to suppress enquiry. He pours himself forth gladly over a thousand things of no importance, while the one grand, infinitely momentous and important question of all—Why is Man, Nature's chief work and care, such a blot on the fair face of creation—that question, so far from considering he will not even permit to be considered.

"No! no! For Heaven's sake, not that. For your life don't open that door of enquiry. Don't attempt to open it. Pass on. Pass on. Open all other doors only not that. Consider everything else, only not that. Make bigger dreadnoughts and ocean liners, fly the air, tunnel Earth's bowels; resolve the ions, tabulate the insects, study more profoundly the construction of the drum of the gnat; investigate everything in the Heavens above and on the Earth beneath or in the depths of Ocean, only not that. Keep that one door well shut and locked. And if anyone seems anxious to open it repel him with ridicule. No one will except the young and ingenuous who are also modest and sensitive to ridicule, say 'Oh! I understand. You wish to resolve the problem of the origin of evil,' and then laugh. You will find that sufficient."

I am not young or inexperienced, or ingenuous and modest and sensitive to ridicule, and I ask you, young men and women of my time, you thinking, observing, considering boys and girls, to retort contempt upon that ridicule, to open boldly that door which the whole world has conspired to keep shut, and to regard this one question as the first and greatest of all questions, nay, the only one which today is worthy of the serious attention of serious-minded young men and women:— How and why have we wandered from the right road, the road planned and made for us by our Maker, and how and by what ways shall we return to it? For we know that we have wandered. Do we not, a good many of us, say so every Sunday, mumbling forth something about lost sheep? "All we like sheep have gone astray. We have followed every one his own way, and there is no health in us."

DUFOUR EDITIONS

Thank you for purchasing this book. For a free catalogue of our other titles that are available from better booksellers, please complete and return this card.

Name: _____

Address: _____

_____

City: _____ State: _____ Zip: _____

Please indicate your areas of special interest:

- ☐ Children's Books
- ☐ Dance, Drama, Theatre
- ☐ History
- ☐ Irish Studies
- ☐ Slavic Studies
- ☐ Gay & Lesbian
- ☐ Literary Criticism
- ☐ Germanic Studies
- ☐ Poetry
- ☐ Religion & Philosophy

- ☐ Scottish Studies
- ☐ Mystery / Crime Fiction
- ☐ Welsh Studies
- ☐ Women's Studies
- ☐ Scandinavian Studies
- ☐ Crafts, Hobbies, Cooking
- ☐ Folklore
- ☐ Other _____
- ☐ Other _____
- ☐ Other _____

1-800-869-5677 • www.dufoureditions.com • info@dufoureditions.com • Fax: 610-458-7103

Dufour Editions
P.O. Box 7
Chester Springs, PA 19425-0007

For our ancestors did at least know and publicly and solemnly confess that they had wandered far from the way, that they were lost. They knew that there was a divine road, knew that they had wandered from it, and believed that it was "Sin" that had caused them to wander from it, and that Sin was universal. And so they solemnly pronounced themselves to be all miserable sinners.

It was no religious hypocrisy at all upon their part, but a deep intuition of a fact: but they could only see the fact through an intervening medium of inherited religious prepossessions. So, Sin came with them to have an almost exclusively theological significance; for presently the plain man who was no theologian and who, too, was beginning to feel doubts about the prevailing religions, found that he could not take Sin quite seriously; it was a matter for the clergy and the more devout of their congregation. The religions have made the word their own, so that, save amongst professedly religious people, the word is not used at all or used in a light bantering sense. Many a man who will grow red in the face with wrath if called a blackguard is rather pleased than otherwise at being referred to as a sinner. Our ancestors succeeded in imposing a theological meaning on a word which signifies crookedness or wrongness, with this absurd result. The ancient Aryan root, Sin, meaning crooked or bent, has come down to us in the Saxon, Sin, Sinner, sinful, and the Latin-English words, sinuous, sinuosities, sinews: derivatives of the Aryan-Latin, Sin, which appears in sinus—a gulf, a bending of the coast line. Note too as we pass that, right, means straight, wrong, crooked; past participle of the verb to wring.

Our ancestors answered the great question—"Why is Man so mad & unhappy?"—by a solemn declaration that it was because he had wandered from the right or straight way, because he had sinned; and I believe that the authors of the Liturgy had the primary meaning of Sin in their minds when they wrote:—"All we like sheep have gone astray."

Those men, wiser than we, knew that they had gone astray, that all their suffering and unhappiness had arisen from their wandering out of the right way; but they confused the right way with their religious traditions and prepossessions. They knew it was there but they saw it not; they could not see it.

And they were right, in a sense, those religious-minded ancestors of ours, in the midst of all their theological confusions. God and Nature, or, if you like, Nature alone, or, if you like, God acting through Nature and, through what is as prophetic as Nature, the divine spirit of Man, made for us, men and nations, a right way; and we are what we are because we have wandered from the right way, sinned, gone astray; and, in consequence, are now not many steps distant from such ruin and destruction as never before overtook the human race.

And I want you, especially you young men and women and serious-minded thinking boys and girls, of whom are many, you with your lives out in front of you to make or to mar, to consider with me what is that right way, that straight way from which we have all wandered, and so far. You will find that this right way is nothing secret, mysterious, concealed, at all. If you can but open your eyes, and, in spite of all the confusing glamours and illusions of the surrounding corrupt and corrupting world; use your natural eyesight, you will see it lying before you at your very feet, in all its beauty and glory, and leading straight and all the way through Paradise! not the poor confined Paradise which was imagined by the Semitic child-mind of the Orient, but the real everlasting, unbounded, indescribably glorious World-Paradise of Heaven and Earth and their countless marvels and wonder, the true Paradise, yours and mine, that cannot be taken from us, lit by shining Suns and fed by blowing winds. What was that little "garden eastward in Eden" compared with this Paradise in which it has pleased God to place us?

TWO.

THE GREAT PSALM.

The light which is one in Heaven is three on Earth. There is the Light that we share with all things, which makes the waves to dance and glitter and the little child to run and shout: the good sunshine. There is the Light of the Intellect, comprehensible always, and the incomprehensible Light of the Spirit whence all the Arts and Literatures and all that is beautiful and loveable in the lives and ways of men. The great Nation will live in the Sunlight, will welcome and use Intellect fearlessly and gladly, and welcome poets, artists, seers, all who in any way represent spirituality.

History show us no such Nation; therefore the great Nation is yet unborn.

We have seen, a little, how Nature was regarded by the intellectual Greek. Consider now, a little, the feeling towards her of the spiritual Hebrew. The most spiritual utterances of the Hebrew genius are the Psalms, and the greatest of the Psalms is the grand 104th.

You are already familiar with it, no doubt. Nevertheless please read it once more with me while I make a few comments. The commentary will be as short as possible consistently with my general purpose.

I. OH, LORD, MY GOD, THOU ART BECOME EXCEEDING GREAT; THOU ART CLOTHED WITH MAJESTY AND HONOUR.

Observe how the Psalmist, like the Author of the Book of Job, is really silent concerning God. After this great invocation he passes straight to that Nature, to the marvellous manifestations, the glorious living raiment of the otherwise Incomprehensible and unknown God. And of that living raiment he celebrates first—Light!

He does so naturally, inevitably, being of the same race and tradition and of the same order of genius as the men to which we owe that first great Chapter of the Bible. Here, too, there is Paradise; and here, too, in the midst of the Paradise, we shall find Man, erect in his innocence—unfallen. Here, too, the first creation is Light.

2. WHO COVEREST THYSELF WITH LIGHT AS WITH A GARMENT, WHO STRETCHEST OUT THE HEAVENS AS A CURTAIN.

The curtain, is of course, the curtain of a tent. The Lord stretches out the Heavens with as much ease as the desert man raises his tent-pole, spreads it out, and makes fast the skirts of it to the driven pegs. In Isaiah this metaphor occurs frequently:—"Who stretches forth the Heavens like a tent."

3. WHO LAYETH THE BEAMS OF HIS CHAMBERS IN THE WATERS, WHO MAKETH THE CLOUDS HIS CHARIOT AND WALKETH UPON THE WINGS OF THE WIND.

In spite of the word "chambers" the metaphor of the tent is, I think, still continued. The tent of Heaven is made sure by beams, colossal tent pegs, driven into the wild waste of waters, amid which the Creator has founded the World-Paradise.

4. WHO MAKETH HIS ANGELS SPIRITS, HIS MINISTERS A FLAMING FIRE.

The Stars, conceived as a fiery living host, the Bene Elohim or Sons of God, are assuredly here celebrated. The Hebrew never believed that the stars were only glittering material particles. Compare: "The stars in their courses fought against Sisera" (Song of Deborah). The Psalmist could not, in such a hymn, by any possibility leave the Stars out of his roll of wonders. In the corresponding and resembling Creation hymn in Job xx viii, the Stars appear exactly at this place in the wonder-roll. See v. 7.

"When the morning stars sang together and all the Sons of God shouted for joy."

The Stars here are the Bene Elohim: the very Sons of God. They sing together and shout for joy. I suspect that the last redactor, afraid of an imputation of Star-worship, veiled the stellar significance of the verse under consideration and obscured the meaning. As it stands it is meaningless. God's angels and ministers would, of course, be spiritual and flame-like.

The Book of Job, especially the concluding chapters, represent the same kind of Hebrew genius as that to which we owe the First of Genesis and this Psalm; the flood-tide of the spirituality of Israel. Then came the ebb, the obscuration, the stony formalism of the Jew,—his gloomy and terrible Messiah fanaticism began to assume control.

The great Nation when it emerges will know no such culminations and melancholy declines. The sun of its genius will be steadfast. The great Nations of history are only its fore-runners and harbingers, their value only prophetic.

5. WHO LAID THE FOUNDATIONS OF THE EARTH THAT IT SHOULD NOT BE REMOVED FOR EVER.

6. THOU COVEREDST IT WITH THE DEEP AS WITH A GARMENT; THE WATERS STOOD ABOVE THE HILLS.

7. AT THY REBUKE THEY FLED; AT THE VOICE OF THY THUNDER THEY HASTED AWAY.

8. THEY GO UP BY THE MOUNTAINS; THEY GO DOWN BY THE VALLEYS INTO THE PLACE WHICH THOU HAST FOUNDED FOR THEM.

9. THOU HAST SET THEM A BOUND THAT THEY MAY NOT PASS OVER, THAT THEY TURN NOT AGAIN TO COVER THE EARTH.

After celebrating the Creator's victory over the primal waste of waters—those sublime labours of which he has only heard—the Psalmist turns now with a keener joy to the roll of all the beautiful things that he knows and loves; turns to that pure fresh uncorrupted Nature which reveals the beauty and love and wisdom of his God. Note the great resemblance between his words and those of the Author of Chapters xxxix and xl of Job; both possibly the work of the same great seer and singer.

10. HE SENDETH THE SPRINGS INTO THE RIVERS; WHICH RUN AMONG THE HILLS.

11. THEY GIVE DRINK TO EVERY BEAST OF THE FIELD. THEREIN THE WILD ASSES QUENCH THEIR THIRST.

12. BY THEM SHALL THE FOWLS OF THE AIR HAVE THEIR HABITATION WHICH SING AMONG THE BRANCHES.

13. HE WATERETH THE HILLS FROM ABOVE; THE EARTH IS FILLED WITH THE FRUIT OF THY WORKS.

14. HE CAUSETH THE GRASS TO GROW FOR THE CATTLE AND THE GREEN HERB FOR THE SERVICE OF MAN THAT HE MAY BRING FOOD OUT OF THE EARTH.

15. AND WINE THAT MAKETH GLAD THE HEART OF MAN; AND OIL TO MAKE HIM A CHEERFUL COUNTENANCE; AND BREAD THAT STRENGTHENETH MAN'S HEART.

The Singer, like the Author of the First of Genesis, will not endure in his glorious Paradise the presence of the slayer and eater of the animals. Man here eats the fruits of the earth and is strong, drinks the juice of the grape and is glad. Both drunkenness and slaughter are equally far from his thoughts. Man is here eating and drinking, but not eating the animals or drinking himself drunk. As to wine, I suppose the essential truth of the matter is this: When men lead the life which Nature means them to lead, Nature herself will cause them to eat and drink to their good, not to their hurt. Healthy people may be trusted to eat or to drink poisons. Meantime observe that the Singer is no ascetic. He loves bodily health and strength, cheerfulness and beauty, stout frames and merry hearts and bright faces.

16. THE TREES OF THE LORD ALSO ARE FULL OF SAP; EVEN THE CEDARS OF LEBANON WHICH HE HATH PLANTED.

17. WHEREIN THE BIRDS BUILD THEIR NESTS. AS FOR THE STORK THE FIR TREE IS HER HOUSE.

The primitive Hebrew did actually worship trees as in some sense the visible form as well as the dwelling place of the Elohim. Of that simple and natural animism of his ancestors the great Psalmist has inherited much. Hence the striking expression, "The trees of the Lord." Compare the oracular response made to David through the Teraphim: "When thou hearest the sound of a going in the mulberry trees."[26] Along with his sublime monotheism our seer combines a profound perception of the divineness of Nature.

18. THE HIGH HILLS ARE A REFUGE FOR THE WILD GOATS; AND SO ARE THE STONY ROCKS FOR THE CONIES.

19. HE APPOINTED THE MOON FOR CERTAIN SEASONS, AND THE SUN KNOWETH HIS GOING DOWN.

The mind of this poet is all-embracing. He loves and celebrates Night also, knows that Darkness, too, is of God, and therefore divine.

20. THOU MAKEST DARKNESS THAT IT MAY BE NIGHT WHEREIN ALL THE BEASTS OF THE FOREST DO MOVE.

21. THE LIONS ROARING AFTER THEIR PREY DO SEEK THEIR MEAT FROM GOD.

22. THE SUN ARISETH AND THEY GET THEM AWAY TOGETHER AND LAY THEM DOWN IN THEIR DENS.

23. MAN GOETH FORTH TO HIS WORK AND TO HIS LABOUR UNTIL THE EVENING.

The Paradise of this Poet is not a walled-in garden carefully separated from the rest of the world, and elaborately prepared by benevolent Elohim to be the abode of human bliss; a childish conception. He treats his great theme like a man. Like a man having eyes to see with, a heart to feel with, and a mind to understand, he sees, feels, and knows that this whole world, which comes momentarily from God, and is sustained by the power of God, and filled with the presence of God, is in fact the true Paradise, and that this Paradise is everlasting; waiting, forever waiting for Man to re-enter and possess. Then, being poet and prophet, he sees imaginatively, prophetically, in the midst of this Paradise, not Man as he is historically, but Man as he ought to be, as God and Nature intended that he should be. He sees Man as Man, and, un-fallen! Sees him in the bright morning, refreshed with sleep, refreshed with—Home! strong and glad going forth into the cheerful sunlight and the pure air, out upon the earth to put forth there creative glad activities, undescribed, until the evening. He does not see him going forth to war, or to rob, or to drive slaves, or to exploit the unlucky or the weak, or to pursue or snare God's innocent creatures. He sees Man going forth to exert in his own person some glad creative activity until the evening.

I am reminded here of a beautiful Greek couplet of verses, the work of the Poetess, Sappho, well worth quoting in this context:

Ἕσπερε πάντα φέρεις 'όσα Φαίνολις 'εσκεδασ' ' Ἀωσ;
Φέρεις ὀίν, φέρεις ἀίγα Φέρεις μάτερι πάιδά.[27]

"O Evening star, thou bringest home all that which the gleaming Dawn has scattered abroad—Home the sheep, and home the goat, and home the boy to his Mother."

For our Psalmist is not alone in his perception and aspiration. Wherever there are true hearts and undepraved minds there is also an unquenchable yearning towards the life which has Home behind it, and, out before it, the great gay undestroyed and indestructible Paradise of the Earth, teeming with the divine life, bathed in divine air, poured over by the Sun. Today in this Paradise a nightmare-haunted being who calls himself Man but is not, has erected his gloomy

[A page of the typescript is missing here.]

25. SO IS THE GREAT AND WIDE SEA ALSO WHEREIN ARE THINGS CREEPING INNUMERABLE, BOTH SMALL AND GREAT BEASTS.
26. THERE GO THE SHIPS, THERE IS THAT LEVIATHAN WHOM THOU HAST MADE TO TAKE HIS PASTIME THEREIN.

The Psalmist is a little vague and mythological about the Sea. He knows that the Sea too is the Lord's, a part of the great Paradise; but He has never been in vital loving relations with it, never personally familiar with its beauty and mystery. The Israelites only held the valleys and highlands of interior Palestine. They were divided from the great Sea by fierce intervening nations, hostile Canaanites and Philistines.

There is a great cosmological significance in his use of the word Leviathan, elsewhere called "Rehab"; elsewhere the "Serpent that is in the Sea"; and, by the more Eastern Semites, Tiamat; the primeval waste world out of which the Creator made the Heavens and the Earth. I could say much on this subject but it would perhaps be out of place. The chief thing to notice here is that, in spite of a certain ancestral terror of the Sea, the Psalmist knows well that the great Sea too is the Lord's and that the terrible dragon within it is in some sense his minister, dread revealer by his will and mind. His world-paradise is all paradise, there is no sin in it or sorrow, anywhere, no Serpent. He remembers indeed the Serpent—how could a Hebrew man forget the Serpent?—but he sees in him a minister and even a glad minister of the supreme will. There is no devil or evil thing anywhere [One or two pages of the typescript are here missing.]

THREE.

AIR AND LIGHT AND THE HEROIC.[28]
(TO YOUNG IRELAND)

Conventionally we speak of the Heroic Period as that which witnessed the emergence and mighty exploits of the Red Branch of Ulster and their gigantic contemporaries of Ulster and their gigantic contemporaries in the other Provinces; but really the Heroic Age never ends. There are always heroes and the heroic; otherwise mankind would die out and leave the earth empty. Wherever that which is good and right and brave and true is loved and followed, and that which is base despised in spite of its apparent profitableness, there the heroic is present. The heroic is not something to talk about, make books about, write poetry about, but something to be put into act and lived out bravely. And I write so because of late years I notice a growing tendency on the part of our young people to talk grandiloquently about the Heroes of Ireland while they themselves, and quite deliberately, lead most unheroic lives.

The Heroic has been here always ever since the Celt first set foot in Ireland, mostly indeed unremembered and uncelebrated, but from time to time shining out resplendently and memorably in certain great classes and orders of Irish mankind. Consider these various famous orders which have exhibited the heroic temper and observe their most notable characteristics.

First came the super-human and semi-divine Heroes of "The Heroic Period", conventionally so called. They were really the children of the gods of our Pagan forefathers, and their story, which has been very much rationalised by the historians, belongs rather to the world of literature and imagination than to that of actual fact.

The young Red Branch Heroes were educated in the open air and the light. There they learned to shoot javelins straight at a mark; the care of horses, their training; the management of the war-chariot and chariot steeds; the art of the charioteer; the use of the sling; practised running, practised swimming in lake, river, or the sea, and grew up and lived men of the Light, of the Air, and of the Field.

War and the preparation for war are distinctly and always open-air occupations; and that is one of the reasons—it is the physical reason—why warlike nations and warlike aristocracies have been, on the whole, so successful and enduring. True, war is murder, and murder is always murder, always a breach of one of Nature's great laws. But there is a greater law than this merely negative one: "Thou shalt not kill." There is the positive counterpart: "Thou shalt Live and be a living cause of Life," and this command cannot be obeyed by Nations who spend the bright day within doors. Life and Light and Air are inseparable.

So, Peace is eternally good: "Blessed are the peace-makers." But the peaceful must be men who are alive and well, not men who are corrupting. Therefore, when a Nation cries "Pax! Pax! War is horrible," and goes indoors it is not long for this world.

What Nation will be the first to preach and proclaim universal peace, declare the devilishness of murder? Not the Nation that flees from the Sun and Wind, and goes indoors and sits at a desk, crying "Pax! Pax!"

Those "beautiful feet upon the mountains"[29] will never be seen by the warrior Nations, must less by the Nation that goes indoors and sits at a desk and makes money—for a while.

The Red Branch were warriors, and, as such, men of the open air and the Light, their lives spent in grand physical activities out of doors.

Finn and the Fianna Eireen come next in the grand roll of our heroic orders. They were essentially not so much warriors as hunters, and, as such, familiar with field and forest, rivers and lakes, mountains and the sea. They lived in the open air and the Light, lived close to Nature and loved Nature well.

Said Finn:—

"I love to hear the cry of the hounds let loose from Glen Rah with their faces out from the Suir, the noise of wild swine in the woods of Mullaghmast, the song of the blackbird of Letter Lee, the thunder of billows against the cliffs of Eyrus, the screaming of sea-gulls, the wash of water against the sides of my ship, the shouting of Oscar and the baying of Bran early in the morning," etc. etc.

They lived in the open air and loved well all the sights and sounds of nature.

Let them pass; Men of the Light and the Air, diffusing from their memory after two thousand years, from their very names, a gracious odour, "the smell of the field which the Lord hath blessed".[30]

The next grand order of heroic Irishmen, though not hitherto thought of in that light, were the founders of the great monastic communities conventionally known as "the Saints". These men are absolutely historic and just as real and actual as ourselves. Also they were Heroes, and the greatest in that kind probably that ever appeared anywhere on the earth's surface down to date. They were born aristocrats, warriors, lords of land and owners of slaves, into whose souls there flashed miraculously the great eternal truth that man ought not to live upon the labours and sufferings and degradation of other people, but that, and especially while young and strong, he ought to sustain himself and others too, by the labour of his own divine hands. Consider that. And so the Hero-Saints of Ireland, kings and sons of kings, great chieftains and great chieftains' sons and near kinsmen, lords of land and exactors of tributes and masters of working slaves went forth and ploughed the earth and sowed it and reaped it, and dug drains through marshes, and reclaimed wildernesses, and made good roads, and planted orchards and gardens, and tended flocks and herds and bees, and built houses and mills and ships, and became weavers and carpenters and shoemakers, and converted waste places into paradises of peace and plenty. For, presently their magazines were overflowing with wealth, wealth which was of their own creation, not bought or acquired by violence, wealth which they scattered freely to all that were in need and to all travellers and visitors, extending to all a limitless and glad hospitality.

Why did those great men and women and secular princes and princesses, scions of a proud and powerful and martial aristocracy, undertake this slaves' work and with such pride and joy? Mainly because they were already proud and brave men, noble and beautiful-souled women, and filled already with a certain heroic ardour. Then as Christians, too, they remembered who it was whom they worshipped and what was his life. So the eternal truth flashed in upon their souls with a blinding glory, blinding them to everything but itself. Has universal History anything to show us like the lives of those early Irish Christians? And so they passed, and our foolish mankind began to make gods and goddesses of them, and to tell silly stories about them, and Ireland's punishment to-day for all that folly is that men are more inclined to laugh at the Saints than to imitate them, and anti-Irish historians like Froude[31] are able to tell us that we Irish have had no historical celebrities at all, only "a few grotesque saints!"

As they pass those Hero-Saints, Irish imitators of their divine Lord, we see again the re-emergence of the old Pagan-Heroic Ideal in our mediæval chieftainry and their martial clansmen, an Ideal whose realisation involved necessarily violence, rapine in many forms, the war cult, the worship of the sword. Let them pass, too, however great and brave. They had at least a Pagan-Heroic Ideal which they bravely followed and in which they honestly believed. Have you any Heroic Ideal, Pagan or Christian, which you believe in as honestly and follow as bravely? The Irish chieftainry and their martial clansmen were essentially warriors, and as such men of the open air and the light.

Next emerge the Protestant Irish landed gentry of Ireland of the eighteenth century, children of the English Conquest, the gentlemen of Ireland, successors of the defeated Chieftains, men whose right to be included in our heroical types and orders will be disputed by no one who remembers that grand heroic spirit exhibited by those settlers and colonists, when, in 1782, in the face of an angry Empire, they put forth their famous and unforgettable "Declaration of Irish Independence," standing in arms, determined and defiant behind their Declaration. Their faults and follies which have been punished by the extreme penalty of extermination will be forgiven or ignored by History, which will remember only that one grand historic act of theirs and the noble spirit from which it sprang. They were not townsmen, indoor men. They were not city gentlemen, but country gentlemen, essentially men of the open air and the light.

You all know the story of the Irish Volunteers, the Convention in the Church of Dungannon—in the Church, observe—the great resolutions then passed, including that which demanded an extension of the civil and political privileges of "our Roman Catholic fellow-countrymen," generosity and magnanimity being an inseparable accompaniment of the heroic temper.

You are not, I think, aware of the strange spiritual force which was driving them and which emanated from Francis Dobbs[32] and his group, a man who, with the heroic temper then so general united the ardour and sincerity of the prophet and the seer. It was he and his friend Col. Irwin who forced the pace and confused the worldly wisdom of the politicians. Dobbs poring over the Book which all nominally accepted as the living word of the living God, found there, or believed he found, veiled under type and figure and mystic numbers, the sure prediction that our Lord's second Coming would be in Ireland, and here the beginning of His kingdom, and that from hence he would go forth, leading the armies of Ireland for the conquest of the world, so that there might be one fold and one shepherd. All this he explained carefully to the Irish House of Commons by whom— and this is a memorable fact—he was listened to with respect, silence and attention.

Historians snigger a little when they come to Dobbs; the men who heard him, who knew his abilities, civil and military, his integrity and sincerity, did not snigger. Dobbs, the noble visionary, was surely nearer the truth of things than we who pray for that Coming, and rising from our knees make a mock of that which has just passed our lips. Remember, there was more than mere mundane patriotic passion in that lightning flash of Irish heroism, gone almost as soon as come, but which, for one moment, seemed to reveal something beyond the power of human thought to express or even of the human mind, at that time, adequately to conceive.

The truth underlying the thought which held Dobbs appears to be this: Wherever there is a vital, intense and active faith in the realisation of that vision of so many prophets, poets, seers, reaching down from remotest times, their line never ending, there the divine idea will begin to assume actuality; and that may be in any country. May be, I trust will be, in this country, in Ireland. Before faith all difficulties disappear, in its fire the very mountains, as we have been told, will melt like wax.

Finally, and for the first time, emerged into visible influence and power a great class and order of Irishmen here always, though concealed, from the beginning, and which will be here to the end, the Irish peasantry, the men of the plough and spade, tillers of the earth and tenders of cattle, a great order always as the strong foundation of all other classes and interests whose grand peasant virtues and strength, derived from the Earth, the Sunlight, and the Air, need no celebration by me. *This great Irish Order is failing to-day, and even failing fast.*

Now, all these heroic types and orders of Irish manhood from the Red Branch to the Peasant of to-day have been open-air men, men who drew into themselves the strength of the earth and the life-giving force of the sunlight and the pure air, and who lived in close and vital touch with Nature, familiar with field and forest and stream, with the plains and hill sides of Ireland. They all led their lives mainly in the open air, which were also lives of strong physical activity in the open air. Such were the Red Branch, and the Fianna of Finn and the Hero-Saints of the sixth and seventh centuries and the chieftainry and the gentlemen of the eighteenth century *and the Peasantry of Ireland, strong and virtuous and renowned, though they are failing to-day, following the landlords.*

The History of Ireland is the History of its heroic types and orders, and the heroic, as our History teaches us, whatever else it may be, is something which is begotten in the open-air and cherished there by the great elemental forces of Nature, and fed and sustained mainly by physical activity in the open air.

You who live contentedly within doors and found your lives, such as they are, upon unmanly effeminate occupations, nursed within doors, ought not, save as an honest preparation for action, presume to talk or write at all about Heroes and the Heroic or about Irish History which, in essence, is nothing else than the history of our heroic types and orders.

Now, the Saints, according as their primal fire burned low, began to sneak into their cloisters and libraries out of the light, and to live on the labours of serfs; and the gentlemen of Ireland, our landlord order, according as they too failed and their natural force abated, retreated into cities, town houses, villa residences and clubs.

To-day our peasantry aim their best thither also, that is citywards, and, as they can't get there, send thither their scions, their boys and girls; held and governed as they are by the huge superstition of our time that it is a grand thing to have money and live without labour on the labour of others. And, it is not a grand thing at all but very mean and vile, and, as an ideal, nothing else than "a blasphemous fable and a damnable deceit".[33]

Now, all these Heroic types fall short of the Ideal, the Ideal which this century and our time present to us. The Red Branch and the Fianna were men of blood. They are not for us, save with great reservations.

The brave chieftainry and their clansmen were, too, men of blood. They, too, are not for us, save with reservations.

The landed gentry lived without labour on the labour of others. They are not for us.

The Hero-Saints, save and except that we cannot be all celibates, are for ever and for us all a grand pattern exemplar and realised Ideal. They lived mainly in the open air and the light working there with their hands at noble and useful and beautiful occupations. Otherwise they worked indoors in their workshops, and on such manly labour, outdoor and indoor, they erected their great spiritual, intellectual, scholarly, and artistic life. None of the other heroical types are for our imitation, save with great reservations. The Hero-Saints are.

They saw that war was wrong, infernal, contrary to Christ's law: they gave their swords to the smiths to be beaten into spades and hatchets. They saw that slavery was wrong, infernal, contrary to Christ's law. They flung away their whips and freed their slaves, and did their own work. So they became great, famous and powerful. Theirs was the greatest effort made in all time to overthrow the dominion of the evil Power which holds mankind in thrall.

They could not conquer, annex and absorb the world, nor did they ever intend to, or even hope to. Their vows of celibacy kept them always a distinct order, and even a small order. *I am looking to you, boys and girls of Ireland, to do this, to do what the Hero-Saints were not able to do, to conquer Ireland first and then the planet.*

The Peasant labours as the Saints laboured; but he labours under compulsion, not freely and joyfully; and he works selfishly, with an eye to the main chance. He does not believe in his own great life.

The peasant does not believe in his own great life, and never did. The fact was noticed by the great poet, Vergil, when he wrote that immortal line addressed to the Italian peasantry of his time: O fortunatos nimium sua si bona norint, which I may perhaps translate: "O fortunate, fortunate beyond words to express, if you could only understand the happiness which is yours."

But they could not; the mere peasant never does.

The Heroic life of our century, of man to-day involves (1) life in the open air and the light; therefore in the country; (2) a life founded upon the useful physical activities, that is to say labour. Observe, I do not say consisting of such activities but founded upon them, as the spirituality and intellectuality, the art and the scholarship of the saints had their base and foundation in such activities. (3) Labour not devoted to money-making, but to the creation and promotion of life and all that makes life worth living.

If you have this Ideal in your souls, if you hold it and believe in it as firmly and absolutely as you hold and are convinced that money is a good thing, you will discover, without any prompting from me or another, the ways and means of reducing the Ideal into practice. Believe in anything with all your whole heart and the difficulties in the way of its realisation melt away like mists before the rising sun.

Think of that life and compare it with the vile effeminate unheroic life to which the world, and for its own purposes, is inviting you to-day. It draws you into its many well-baited and alluring traps, and kills you there, after a while, and after it has squeezed out of you all it wants.

The Heroic Ideal of our century, of a time when no young man of understanding can believe any more in stealing, robbing, and killing, can be no other than that of our Irish Hero-Saints, only, leading some such manly open-air life, you must fall in love and marry, and multiply and replenish the earth.

Armed with this faith, nothing can stop you, nor can any limits be assigned to your advance.

The practical outcome of our historical review is this. If you desire to lead a brave and manly life, you will in one way or another, probably by purchase, secure possession of a sufficient area of your native land, and there create a self-maintained society founded upon those manly physical, creative activities which are exerted mainly in the open air and the light. If you determine to do that, everything that lives will be on your side; God and Nature and Man will help you; Sun and Wind, and Earth, and Water will co-operate with you and be your friends and allies.

Such a Society will be a Nation, and such a Nation the whole world will not be able to put down and will not want to put down.

I know well the strength of the net in which you are enmeshed. I know that it is stronger, far stronger, than even you think it is; but I know, too, that if you are determined to break through it you can. Here for your encouragement I give you a snatch of song which I read once casually in some newspaper and have never forgotten. It may be a help to you when ways seem intricate, prospects gloomy, and high spirits sink and flag:—

> "They ringed him round with a fence of steel,
> And they thought that at last he was under their heel,
> But the lion is up and hath rended his net,
> And he's out in the Open—De Wet, De Wet." [34]

FOUR.

NATIONS AND NATIONS.

Don't allow yourselves to be bullied out of your natural per-
ceptions by these vast unwieldy, ungoverned and ungovernable
modern Empires which call themselves Nations and are not,
and which are held together, not by a common life, but
mainly by bullets. All the noblest Nations, and when at their
noblest, have been surprisingly, astonishingly small as to territorial extent. If you have in you a spirit such as was theirs you
might build up a Nation, even a great Nation upon a territory
across which, from one side to another for healthful exercise
or for fun, you might run or walk before breakfast in the
morning. I speak by the book. History teems with examples,
not only of noble things done and grand characters emerging
from minute States, but of great and flourishing populations
maintained upon exceedingly small territories. If you know this
rightly, you will not, as intending Nation-builders, despise
even one 20 acre field. You don't understand as yet at all what
the Earth is willing and eager to do for Man when Man has
not forgotten his manhood. Read what here follows with the
assistance of a map of Ancient Greece. If you have none
such buy one; also a Map of Ireland, and with the scale in
miles marked at the foot of each.

On the West of Greece, off the Coast of Epirus, observe
the little straggling crooked Island of Corcyra, some 30 miles
long, indeed, but averaging four or five in breadth. The little
Island boasted some fertile valleys and scanty plains good for
corn and the olive tree, but was and is, in the main,

mountainous and barren. Its area, all told, rough and smooth, is hardly greater than that of one of our Irish Baronies, of which about ten go to a County. The County of Meath has 19 Baronies, all rich alluvial soil, any one of them worth perhaps half a dozen Corcyras.

In the fifth century B.C., this little barren Island was the habitat of a great independent Sovereign Greek Power. Consider its resources in wealth, materials and in men.

The war fleet alone of Corcyra, apart from her vastly larger mercantile marine, numbered 120 triremes. Now a trireme was a great brazen-beaked galley propelled by 170 oars; three bands or rows of 25 oars on each side; and, besides the oarsmen, carried ten soldiers and 20 supernumeraries, cooks, carpenters, attendants and officers. So the crew of a trireme was 200 men. The little rocky Island, therefore, employed a fighting sea service of 24,000 men. Think too of the docks where this navy was constructed and maintained and of all the hands employed there. Then she had an army as well, some 5,000 men at the least, for Corcyra Queened it on the land as on the sea, and had many settlements, trading stations and colonies scattered along the Epirote coast, treaties to maintain there and friendly tribes to protect.

As we look at the little straggling mountainous Island all this seems like a miracle; but was no miracle at all to the contemporaneous Hellenes to whom the spectacle of great Nations sustaining their greatness upon little scraps of the Earth's surface was quite common.

Consider Corinth, another contemporaneous great naval State and Nation. I may add that both Corcyra and Corinth were members of the same noble Dorian Division of the Hellenic race; so, too, were the Spartans.

The Peloponesian war began in a struggle between Corcyra and Corinth for the sovereignty of the Corinthian gulf and the control of the trade routes leading to the West. In this fighting the Corinthians took the sea with 150 triremes; that is with a war-fleet manned by 30,000 men. They had besides an army of some 10,000 hoplites, trained foot-soldiers, all in armour,

and a vast mercantile marine. Now the territory of which
Corinth was the capital, measured about 10 miles by 20; so
about the size of one of our larger Irish Baronies. Remember
all the docks and ship carpenters behind a fleet of such
dimensions. At the same time the Athenians maintained a war
fleet of 300 triremes, manned therefore by a force of 60,000
men, furnished altogether out of their own Athenian and
Attic resources; that is, not by their allies and subject states.
Unlike the Corcyreans and Corinthians, the Athenians possessed in their territory of Attica a huge hinterland all united
as a single State under the leadership of Athens. For Athens
indeed we must admit the huge hinterland. But, now compare
this huge hinterland with one of our Irish Counties, Limerick,
Tipperary, or Meath, and you will find the Irish County to be
greater in size.

Then, the Irish County is probably three times as fertile as
Attica ever was, more adapted by nature for the production
and maintenance of wealth and men. Attica took the field
against the first Persian invasion with 10,000 men, first-rate
men too, as the event proved, and defeated the Persians at
Marathon.

Later, when the Athenians sought to extend their Empire
in the West, they sent an army of 40,000 men into Sicily.

The Athenians did such things having for their support a
territory no greater than an average Irish County and not
nearly as fertile.

Nations—can any one doubt it?—became great through
greatness of soul, not through expansion. This is what I want
you to understand. Understand this and you won't despise a
single Irish field.

Turn now to the Map of the Peloponesus and consider
renowned Sparta and the heroic brood that emerged there in
the small valley watered by the Eurotus, lying between the
mountain ranges of Taygetus on the West and Parnon on the
East, and blocked on the North by the mountainous highlands
of classic Arcadia. You will find that, as to territorial expansion, the smallest of our Irish Counties, Carlow, has as great

an area. Also spurs and projecting barren highlands from those mountain ranges invaded and occupied a good part of that Lacedemonian vale. Sparta proper was a group of allied villages in the midst of Lacedemon. These villagers, who were about 10,000 men, but all warriors, and representing everything that was best in the great Dorian race, gradually brought under their government all that Lacedemonian vale, and, afterwards, Messenia on the West and the country beyond Parnon on the East, so establishing a Spartan Empire with themselves as the ruling aristocracy of the same. Now, measure this Spartan Empire from Sandy Pylos on the West to rocky Prasiae on the East and from the Arcadian highlands on the North to the single little Spartan port of Gythium on the South. We may leave out the rocky prongs which southern Peloponesus thrust out into the Aegean. You will find that its dimensions are not greater than those of Meath, Limerick, or Mayo. Then, unlike our rich Irish Counties, that marvellous Spartan Empire with the handful of brave Spartans in the midst of it consisted largely of mountainous and rocky heathery highlands only good for goats.

This Empire, nevertheless, in spite of its scarcity of fertile plains and valleys, held an immense and even wealthy population of Greek men who were policed and regulated and held in submission and discipline by that handful of Spartans. These last then had need to be what they were, men as hard as the knots of the holm oaks of their native Taygetus, of a temper like steel, compact, well gathered together, silent, perfectly disciplined, loyal to each other and to their Gods and their laws and their captains. Such was the work that the destinies had cut out for them and which they were compelled to undertake and carry through at their peril. Hence the Spartans; and hence their great name and fame which have gone abroad into all lands and can never be forgotten. The word, Spartan, in every language suggests a certain ideal hardness and hardihood and manly asceticism. It is forgotten that they were Idealists too, impassioned lovers of the beautiful. The great populousness of those little classic independent

States and diminutive Empires is not to-day recognised; but it should be, and especially by you who cherish the thought of becoming yourselves Nation-builders. If the right spirit be present, you need only a very little land and few material resources for that purpose; though indeed, much, in fact everything, underlies that little word—"if". For Mind is everything, Matter nothing, in comparison.

The second and far more formidable invasion of Greece by the Persians was, upon land, defeated and rolled back to the Hellespont by the Spartans under their King Pausanias at the battle of Plataea. Pausanias led into the great battle 8,000 Spartan men, 10,000 free Lacedaemonian subjects of the Spartans, called Perioeci,—that is, neighbours or near-dwellers, and 35,000 armed Helots! Observe that the theatre of war was far away in the North of Greece and that the 8,000 Spartan aristocrats were not afraid to go upon that distant campaign and into a battle against a vastly superior number of Persians accompanied by 47,000 men, their subjects, 35,000 of whom were their slaves, Helots, whom, according to old stories, they treated like dogs, murdered at pleasure, made drunk as object lessons for their boys, etc. etc. The Spartans were a very exclusive people who did not at all relish the presence amongst them of irresponsible and undisciplined aliens. Such stories to their discredit would naturally grow up and be circulated amongst those who desired but could [not] attain to intimacy with them. Are not exclusive people even to-day the subject of ill-natured tales?

Now, it is unreasonable to suppose that the Spartan government would or could send to the front and at a great distance from their base every subject of military age. We may assume, I think, for we can only guess that the 55,000 men led into the battle by Pausanias represented a total manhood of probably more than three times that number, and that therefore the full population of the Spartan Empire at this date exceeded a million.

I take the foregoing numbers from the notes in Walford's translation of Aristotle's Economics,[35] Bohn's series, p. 63.

The Perioeci were altogether 30,000 men, of whom only a third, or 10,000 were brought out, and probably not a fourth or a fifth of the total manhood of the Helots. We are, therefore, justified in supposing that the total manhood of the whole Spartan Empire was at least 200,000, and therefore the total population over a million.

Again, compare that little sterile mountain-traversed Empire as to mere territorial extent with one of our great fertile Irish Counties and you will find yourself driven to the conclusion that, in spite of their Paganism, something in the nature of a divine blessing rested upon that Spartan land which seems to be rather absent to-day from our great fertile deep-loamed Irish Counties, be the cause what it may. If Ireland, in proportion to her size and fertility, were populated in the same degree, what would our population be? We number only a little more than four millions. Therefore, we need one of our vast rich Christian Irish Provinces to sustain a population equal in number to that which the little Heathen Spartan Empire maintained in the days of Leonidas, and maintained in comfort and prosperity, in a condition of manly opulence and physical and moral efficiency.

For, depend on it, it was not starvelings or an army of discontented and unhappy and vicious men whom Pausanias led into that great battle and at whose head he overthrew the vast hordes of the world-conquering Persian.

Note now another fact which I am particularly anxious that you, as intending Nation-builders, should consider and reflect upon. Unlike the Corinthians, Corcyraeans and Athenians, unlike all the other surrounding Nations, the Spartans had no foreign commerce. There is the wonder! They became great famous and powerful without trade. The Spartans did not like traders and their ways, regarding them as, on the whole, a dishonest class of men: therefore dangerous, especially so if let loose amid a disciplined primitive community like theirs. The Spartan Ephors knew something of Tyre, Carthage, Corinth, the Peiraens, and the other great commercial ports of the world and the strange long-shore populations, male and female, which swarmed in such ports, and did not like them. They feared them. So, the Spartans determined to make their little Empire self-sustaining and to live on their own resources according to a political economy of their own. They saw another kind of political economy at work in the Mediterranean. They saw the Professors and practitioners of that political economy caring nothing about right and wrong, nothing about the good and the beautiful, caring little about even their Gods and Heroes, but caring a great deal about buying in the cheapest market and selling in the dearest. Which, indeed, is no sublime modern discovery at all, being just as old as sin. So, the Mediterranean merchant-princes, though longing greatly to do so, were never able to get a footing in the little Spartan haven of Gythium, or convert it into a roaring, commercial emporium. Gythium, as a rule, held nothing but some fishing boats and coasting boats, and two or three Spartan State triremes. Sometimes a great sea-prince with his laden merchant-men and his protecting war galleys put into Gythium, and proposed trade with the natives. He felt certain that with these unsophisticated natives he could buy cheap, and sell dear, and practise with brilliant success both great provinces of his simple political economy.

He had for sale, handsome boys and lovely white-skinned rosy girls from the Black Sea; dark-eyed Hebrew maidens—he bought them at Askelon from the Philistines—and would sell cheap; beautiful glowing Tyrian purples; goodly Babylonish garments; Frankincense, Myrrh and spices from Arabia; sponges from Patmos, very close in texture; pearls and diamonds; superior Chian and Samian wines; etc., etc., very cheap all; and would buy their wool, skins, corn, oil, and pay by exchange or gold down, pure Aeginetan coinage: no alloy. For your fine Spartan boys and girls he would pay a very high price.

Presently a plain-looking middle-aged man wearing a rough cloak and in his hand a big untrimmed oak stick or knobby blackthorn would come riding down to Gythium out of the North, on his pony, or more probably stepping down firmly on his two feet, a man of an iron frame, if of gentle manners and looking the King that he was arriving he explained to the seductive Sea-Prince that this was Sparta, and that although his wares were, doubtless, very good and very cheap, yet that the Spartans had been for many generations in the habit of producing for themselves everything that they required. He also suggested very politely that the Sea Prince, with his rich fleet, had best not waste valuable time here but row off to the Argolid or Miletus, or to the Corinthian Gulf where he would find many Hellenes as eager as himself to buy and sell; but that here foreign trade was forbidden by the Laws. The middle-aged man with the rough home-spun cloak and big stick—it was his Sceptre!—expressed himself with singular clearness but very courteously; gracious manners were a second nature with Spartans. But there was no mistaking his meaning.

Indignant and disappointed, the great Sea-Prince dashed on board and trumpeted his orders. A thousand oars shot out from the galleys' black sides, and the rich fleet moved out through the haven's mouth into the blue Aegean, leaving a great white track in its trail, aiming towards some country less utterly barbarous.

The barbarous people nevertheless, knew very well what they were about. The Spartans had, of their own, plenty of corn and oil and fruit, and a good rough, wholesome Spartan wine. They wove their own wool and flax, and tanned and dressed their own leather. They dug iron out of their mountains and hammered it to steel or metal which they loved well being all warriors.

Exit Civilisation with a devil in its belly, contemplated silently from the shore by the middle-aged man with bright steel-cold eyes and his face like a rock.

For gold the Spartan had no use, or for silver. Having no foreign commerce, they did not need the precious metals; their iron money served well for the facilitations of their internal exchangings. So values could be, and were settled by custom, and the dishonest[y] and demoralisation attendant on unrestrained haggling avoided. For example, the Spartan

gentleman did not and could not rack rent. His Helots paid
him half the produce of his lands. I may mention that
contemporaneously the free Athenian or Attic agriculturalist
paid his lord five sixths of the produce of his land; also the
Helot was no chattel slave, not the property of his lord, like
the other slaves of the ancient world: he was owned by the
State not by his lord, and even the State could not sell him.

Sparta kept ancient Civilisation at a good arm's length, but
ancient Civilisation was literary and witty, and took a good
literary revenge.

The Spartans did not need the dubious gifts of that surrounding Civilisation. For building their houses they had plenty
of stone; while for roofing them the beautiful Eurotas supplied
an abundance of reeds and rushes. These were gathered
gratefully; for Eurotas was a live god and liked being spoken
to and praised and thanked. Every little boy and girl knew the
romance of Eurotas his lovely daughter Sparta, and how
Lacedaemon, the Prince, fell in love with and married her in
the gleaming dawn of history when anything might have happened; provided only it was beautiful enough and appealed to
the heart and imagination or the fancy of the most believing
and imaginative race on earth.

They had marble for their beautiful Doric temples, and
from which to hew their still mostly an-iconic, that is, formless
undefined symbols of the Gods. A degenerating Civilisation had
not yet given them Gods almost exactly resembling themselves. The genius of the Greek was failing when he made
marble men and called them Gods.

They had abundance of fuel in the forests that clothed the
sides of Parnon and Taygetus. In short within their little
Empire they found everything that a brave and virtuous people
required. And, as for handsome boys and lovely girls—, why,
they were themselves producing at the time the very finest
boys and most beautiful girls in the world, and felt no desire
to sell them for goodly Babylonish garments or for gold down.

Sometimes, not being at all fools or even narrow-minded
they did invite distinguished and desirable aliens to come

and live with them, and on such occasions made very good selections. So they brought in the lame man Tystaens who composed Tyrtaean war songs for their young braves, songs that helped the State in the Messenian wars more than would ten thousand trained Hoplites. Then out of that dangerous Asiatic highly civilised Lydia—the Ephors were not afraid—they brought in the Lydian poet, Alcman, to make hymns for them and choral songs; hymns and songs calculated to bring the Spartan people and their Gods into nearer and dearer relations.

Once when they were threatened with collapse through internal dissensions they sent for and brought in as the greatest discoverable pacificator and reconciler of angry men, him who was the most renowned Musician of the then known world. Terpander, the lesbian, with his "Seven-stringed lyre"

Music, the service of all Apollo's daughters, included then everything that was beautiful and lovely and of good report and not sweet sounds alone. Terpander, with his music alone harmonised the disturbed Spartan State stilling the angry waters; and his great music lasted for centuries on Eurotas' banks unchanged; for the Spartans having proved a thing to be good would not suffer any alterations, being the most conservative of mankind and above all, loyal to the Laws. The Laws of Sparta were un-written. That is, they were not written on parchment or on brass, but were written deep in the hearts of every Spartan boy and girl, and stayed there.

Great Nations don't write their Laws; base Nations do.

But some one may object, "If the Spartans were as perfect as you say, how did they ever break down and come, as they finally did, to imbecillity shame and sorrow?"

But I never said that they were perfect. Perfection did not and could not belong to men who wore on their hips a bit of steel with which to bore through the bodies of other men, and let out the divine life in streams of streaming blood. Men who appropriated the holy Earth and by force and violence compelled other men to cultivate the same for them as their slaves; men who deprived other men of their manhood and established an iron system of castes; men who believed so little in themselves, in their own virtue and native manhood that they were afraid of two beautiful and innocent metals and kept them out by force; men who were afraid of strangers and, therefore, inhospitable, extremely so; men who were afraid of philosophers and students of the marvellous ways of Nature.

No, I never said they were perfect, or thought it. I think of them rather as wonderfully fine boys who made a grand attempt to conquer the wicked old world, but did not know enough to succeed. Add what Christ knew to what Lycurgus and the Spartan Ephors knew and you will make a Nation which will take the devil by the throat and strangle him. You understand now the astonishing smallness as to area of renowned powerful and populous Greek Sovereign States. But much more, pointing in the same direction, remains behind which I now bring forward for the encouragement of all brave Nation-builders.

See now the little Island of Lesbos "Where burning Sappho loved and sung," and where Alcaeus praised her in Alcaeic verses; "The dark-haired spotless, sweetly smiling Sappho." It lies off the Asiatic Coast near the entrance to Propontis or the Bosphorus, and its area is 25 miles by 25; about one fourth of our County of Mayo. Now, in the fifth and preceding centuries Lesbos was divided between Five Sovereign Greek States. There was Mitylene, Methymna, Antissa, Eresus and Pyrrha, with her magnificent land-locked harbour. Here Achilles took captive the beautiful maid, Briseis, who became a cause of contention between himself and Agamemnon; and so the cause too of the greatest poem yet written by Man; the Iliad.

Each of these five States or Nations had its own army and its own navy; its own State cult, and, over all, its own protecting God. Each of them, even the smallest, was as independent and self-governing as France, only a great deal more so; as proud and self-reliant, and with a better right, as was England when Campbell[36] wrote song:—

"Britannia needs no bulwarks, no towers along the steep."
I say "better right" for none of these five Sovereign Lesbian

States, while rejoicing in her own freedom, a self-government and absolute independence of foreign control, cared at all to bully her neighbours or played the termagant of the waters.

Why have historians and philosophers forgotten or deliberately ignored the grand political lesson taught by Greece to mankind? Look well at this Island of Lesbos with her five Sovereign States and consider that the area held by each could not have been greater than that comprised in a few of our Irish Parishes. Then, one of them, Mitylene, produced such great personages as Sappho, Alcaeus, Terpander, Pittacus, the brave "Tyrant", enumerated amongst "the Seven Wise men of Greece," and also other famous worthies. Great Nations are made by greatness of soul not by huge territories or by congregated vast hordes of the mean and vulgar. Take here one slight instance of the magnanimous spirit, which animated the people of those Aegean Greek islands. See the little island of Chios, famous for its Chian wines. Here a funeral tablet has been unearthed bearing this inscription:—

"We, Bitto and Phainis lie here together. We were poor women and old; but the first as to blood and birth. We used to sing the histories of the Demigods."

Old age and poverty could not drive high thoughts out of those hearts of fire. They remembered their heroes and were content and proud; sang glad songs about them to the accompaniment of their seven-stringed Chian lyres. I wish we had a few such beautiful old Irish ladies to-day, to make things hum a little in this our near-songless land. And—as to the Heroes, just one word here which is of the nature of an aside. The Heroes are not behind us, but before. They are out in front.

Here too flourished the hereditary School of Ionian Greek bards, who called themselves Homeridae, or children of Homer; and here no doubt and by that poetical genius (it is Grote's opinion) a great deal of the Iliad and Odyssey was actually composed. The two beautiful old ladies, Bitto and Phainis were doubtless of the family.

And the same blessing rested upon little Chios too which enfolded the rest of the Greek world in its great age evidenced in an astonishing material prosperity. Poor barren little Chios in war time took the Aegean with 70 triremes; that is a sea service of 14,000 men. Valiant Chian men fired up to do great things for their country by songs, and hero tales, such as those which Bitto and Phainis used to sing. And as brave men never come save through good women, let me remark here before I pass that it was a boast of the Chians that for 700 years, there had been no recorded instance of adultery in their beautiful island. Whether literally true or not the Chians made their brag.

The King of Historians, Thucidydes, has singled out the little island for a special praise.

"No Nation," he writes, "so far as I know, except the Chians and the Lacedemonians have observed modesty in the midst of prosperity."

That is, balance, moderation, with an under-feeling of manly shame. The true Greek, the true human feeling concerning Nemesis. The divine wrath which dogs the imperious progress of the prosperous; the successful and the proud.

The area of that heroic little island is some 30 miles by 12. Seven or ten such States might be carved out of one of our vast Irish Counties.

FIVE.

THE GREEK POLIS.

When we read of the Athenians, the great deeds they did, their great men and great masterpieces, we think of them inevitably as citizens of the famous City of Athens, "the eye of Greece", the "fair and renowned and with violet crowned", most beautiful and illustrious of all Cities. We read how the Athenians fought and conquered the world-conquering Persian at Marathon, and again on the sea at Salamis and Mycale; and how they made and again lost the great Athenian Empire, lording it over a thousand subject States, from Sardinia to the Tauric Chersonese; and how they created another Empire in the mind of Man, which they have not lost, nor ever will. Then, naturally, we think of all these great things as done by the citizens of the famous city by the Ilisus; presided over by the Acropolis and the menacing august figure of Athena.

But the name is a misnomer, and not a harmless one; it has seriously distorted historical perspective. How mis-leading and confusing, for example, would history hereafter be, should historians universally write of the British Empire as Londonian; and of Shakespeare, Byron, Burns, Wordsworth, Shelley and Carlyle as great Londonians! The Athenians of history were really the men whose limbs were made by the good Attic soil and clear transparent air of that sunny classic land, which reached from Cithaeron on the North to Cape Sunium on the South; and from the waters of the Euripus on the East to the Saronic and Corinthian Gulfs on the West. There, embrowned by shining suns and blowing winds, their bodies hardened for war and the strenuous marine labour of the oar, by manly physical activities pursued in the open Air and the Light, dwelt the men whom history name the Athenians.

It was they, the men of Attica, who foiled the Persian at Marathon, and rammed and smashed his mighty navies. The men of Marathon were not the little handful of hoplites sent out of Athens, the city proper, to share in the famous fight. The morale and the physique; the courage and the corporal strength and activity and the clear-seeing martial intelligence which then saved Greece and Europe were not bred in any town but in the plains of Attica, the valleys along the mountain sides of Cithaeron, Parnes and Hymetius, under Sunium's marble steep, on the banks of the Attic streams and the shores of her all-but surrounding seas. Nay, it is a historic fact that the great Athenians of the great age of Athens were, in fact, sprung from the class or order whom we would now call country gentlemen. Theseus and Codrus; Pisistratus and his sons, Miltiades, Aristiades, Aristides, Pericles, Thucydides, Conon and Cimon were all of this class, essentially men of the open air.

Cleon was the first city man seemingly to arrive at power in the State; and his ascent synchronised with the beginning of the downfall. Then, we may be quite certain that even Cleon's big frame and stout heart and resounding voice were not made in any counting house in Athens or the Peiraeus.

The Athenians of the great period were the Ionian Greeks of the Territory of Attica, men of the open country; children of the Light and Air; of the Sun and Wind.

Consider for a moment the history of this classic region. Much of the most vital importance to us to-day will be learned from it; I say to us and to-day because I am not really thinking of the past, but of the present; and not of the ancients who are dead, but of you who are alive, and with life's great problems staring you in the face.

At Marathon the Attic host was commanded by ten Polemarchs, or war captains; each leading his own separate division of 1000 men. Why ten commanders? Because the now federated Nation which was beginning to be known as the

Athenians, had in the preceding centuries consisted of ten independent Sovereign States. (I am aware that Grote[37] makes them twelve.) Those ten Sovereign Attic States had drawn together and confederated voluntarily, and made Athens their centre of general assembly. They drew together, first and before all else, for religious purposes, and in order so to worship more solemnly and splendidly the common protecting Gods of all the States. Afterwards they combined politically, but retained, each of them, large powers of local autonomy. Hence the ten Polemarchs. The Athenians of history were the ten federated States of Attica. Of such independent Attic States there was Athens herself with her surrounding territory; Eleusia, famous for the Mysteries; Acharnae; Braurn on the East Coast—the great Pisistratus was a Brauronian; the Marathonian Tetrapolis or four citied State, which had for its God the Hero, Theseus, and five others. Athens was but one of the ten. Moreover, the State of Athens was not the little walled City of that name beside the Ilisus, but the territory of which Athens was the Capital and which lay along both shores of the Cephisus. So the Athenian contingent of 1,000 hoplites consisted mainly of men of the field and vineyard, men of the country who were seldom seen in the City save on market days and holy days. The so-called Athenian contingent was but a tenth of the ten thousand, who converged out of all Attica upon Marathon; and probably not a tenth of the Athenian thousand were properly townsmen. They were the vineyard-dressers and olive-growers; the farmers, labourers and gentlemen of the Cephisian plain. The ten Polemarchs commanded the armies of the territorial divisions of Attica which had been ten Sovereign States and which had only parted with their absolute independence for certain purposes. The Attic people were not so much a Nation as a Nation of Nations, ten separate independent Nations. Consider now the area of that famous country and you will find it to be about half that of our County of Mayo! Therefore, had the Greeks, when in their prime, colonised Ireland they would have carved the territories of 20 independent Sovereign States out of that one County.

To us, fools of our eyes, who think that national independence needs millions of square miles for its sustenance and that a Nation must consist necessarily of millions of people all this seems strange enough, stranger still than that the Athenian fame and name and Empire should have been sustained by a territory, a great deal less than half of our County of Cork and perhaps not a third as fertile. But something stranger remains behind.

Each of those ten Ionian-Greek Attic States had itself grown to be what it was through a prior voluntary drawing together and confederation of still smaller independent States called Demes. Demos means a People. Whence our words Democracy, Demagogue, etc. Now an average of five Demes—Demoi or Peoples—went to the formation of one of those ten territorial divisions. Every Deme was a *Demos*, or separate People, also a *Polis* or self-governing State. For the Greek word Polis signifies far more than a City. It means a City and its Territory; both in conjunction, forming an independent State. So, amongst the territorial Divisions just enumerated you will find one, the Marathonian Tetrapolis; which means the Four-citied confederation of the plain of Marathon.

The Marathonian Tetrapolis, one of the ten States of Attica, was itself formed by a free voluntary confederation of four Demes or Peoples; each of which, a fact certified by the name Tetrapolis, consisted of a Polis or City-State; a City and its sustaining territories. You may call the City a village, if you please; and the Polis or City-State a village commune, if you like. It was certainly that. But the grand thing to remember is that each of those village communes assumed the proud title of Polis, and exercised all the rights and powers external and internal of a Sovereign and independent Greek State, brooking no interference with its affairs foreign and domestic. It had its own temple and State cult and religion, its own protecting God. Theseus or Heracles or Erectheus or another; its own laws and constitution and national banner and army; and filled every man, woman and child amongst them with a passionate Greek devotion to their own God and their own small country.

The Deme was a Sovereign State and independent Nation, and confirmed in its independence by its own resolution; by Greek International law; by the sanction and protection of the Gods, against whom it was an unspeakable crime and foul impiety for any Deme to violate a neighbour's boundaries and remove his land-marks. "Cursed be he who removeth his neighbour's land-marks",[38] was international law in Greece as in the Holy Land when the Greek was in his prime.

We were not taught this at school and college; nor is it yet taught there but scholars are now so well aware of it that it has begun to get into the Encyclopaedias. I quote this from the latest and most popular, "Deme", "a district of Attica inhabited by a tribe forming an independent community. These communities by degrees united into larger States." Tribe is hardly the correct word for the Deme, though always a Polis or full State, was not always exactly a Clan or Tribe. "Five Demes sent to the formation of one Trittys of which there were ten. Each Deme retained its own officers and property and Agora" (i.e. a meeting place for self-government.)

Therefore, in the centuries that preceded Marathon there was a time when Attica consisted of ten Sovereign States; independent and self-governing autonomies, and beyond that again a time when the land was held by some fifty independent States; and all these so friendly and fraternal, and liking each other so well that they grew together and coalesced voluntarily into ten States, which ten, under the impulse of some man of genius—Theseus or another—voluntarily coalesced into one, forming a combined Attic Nation, known to history as "the Athenians".

The Deme, like the ten later confederations known to history, was held together, and maintained its organic unity, not so much through the bond of common blood or of common interests as through the bond of a common religion. For it is an historical fact, explain it as you may, that the primitive Greek Nation was made and maintained by its God. Those mysterious relations between the individual man and his Nation and his National God cannot be understood at all by us moderns who are outside that magic circle. Those strange mysterious relations between the Nation and its God we find revealed, somewhat, in the early literature of Israel. But the general fact is certain. The primitive Nation everywhere was held together by its God.

The true Greek State was a religious rather than secular Community; a Church and a State in vital organic union, but a great deal more a Church than a State. It is very important to remember this. To the men, women and children of those little Attic Demes, their religion was ten times more important and more interesting and more delightful than any province of secular affairs. Their great joy of life was their religion and the festivities, dramas, processions, sacrifices and arts which grew out of it. What their God, his Ark, Tabernacle, Oracles, joyful Communional feasts, was to the primitive Israelites; that and even more, was its God to the little primitive Greek Nation; for he was not only their invisible potent friend, Captain and guardian, but their actual physical ancestor as well. He was their loving father, and they his most loving and loyal children. The blood of their immortal sire flowed in their veins.

In the terms of which I write they did not think either lewdly or lightly at all of that holy and mysterious union of an immortal God or divine hero with a mortal maid, from which they themselves were sprung. It was a sacred mystery. In later times that primitive simplicity and naivete, earnest devoutness and unquestioning faith yielded before the incoming of unpitying relentless knowledge. The Greek lost his religion and along with it his original patriotism and happiness, his pride and his power. The long slow wave of accumulating life broke at last in splendour and sound, and breaking died.

That multitude of independent Attic Nations were able to live side by side, with mutual respect and mutual regard. We in our twentieth century intellectual pride and arrogance making our violence-loving selves the measure of mankind cannot but believe that primitive Attica with its 50 independent separate, yet contiguous Nations must have been the bloody theatre of continual and desolating warfare. But that was not so. No tradition of any such bloody time survived for the base historian to gloat over. Moreover, the fact that those groupings of States, first into ten Attic autonomies and then into a single Attic Nation, brought about by voluntary coalition forbids the presumption of a preceding age of violence. There was then, a time when Attica, a country about half the size of the county of Mayo, and not nearly so fertile; was the habitat of fifty independent Greek States; Sovereign Peoples, each with its Capital and territory, dwelling together in a friendly and fraternal manner and therefore gladly and happily. Now if we to-day believe in our Religion, ought we not to be pleased? Recall certain sentences which we hold to be divinely inspired.

"How sweet and pleasant a thing it is—brethren to dwell together in unity!"[39]

"How beautiful on the mountains are the feet of him who cometh proclaiming peace!"[40]

"Blessed are the peacemakers."[41]

To-day our educators, and now for a long time, have been teaching ingenuous youth that man is naturally greedy, rapacious, violent, that his natural state is a state of war, rapine, exploitation, while, at the same time, they, or a good many of them, profess to believe that the words which I have quoted are divine. For men can easily become so insane as to believe contradictories. Don't believe them. Man is by nature the most social of all the living creatures on the face of the Earth; that is, the most kindly, friendly and affectionate; and, now and then, and here and there, has been able to shake off the nightmare of evil by which he is oppressed, and exhibit himself as God and Nature and his own Divine Spirit have made him. Such were the Greeks in the great age of the Hellenic race.

Your first mental impulse on reading what I say will be, I know, one of scepticism; nay, of angry and contemptuous scepticism. It will disturb the balance of ideas to which you are accustomed and which, by familiarity, has grown acceptable.

And is it not an odd and even ludicrous thing that you should be pleased to hear that you are by nature a scoundrel and thief and murderer, and are displeased to hear it even suggested that you are naturally upright, magnanimous and affectionate?

The fact is that all the great powerful and dominating interests, which, collectively, we may call the World, maintain their dominion by keeping you in that state of mind. As long as you believe in the natural scoundrelism of man, so long you and they in conjunction will uphold the reign of force and laugh away the thought of peace and security maintained by anything else than force and violence. Then, Essayists, Encyclopaedists, Newspaper Editors, Professors, romantic historians, a mighty crowd of talking and writing people keep saying till it has become a kind of axiom:—"Man is eternally a scoundrel; therefore force is an eternal necessity."

In those ages all Hellas, and not Attica only, was occupied by minute self-governing Nations, each with its little territory and capital. Search anywhere, everywhere and you will find the little Autonomies.

Keats, with the intuition of genius, perceived the fact and loved it.

Recall these beautiful lines from his "Ode to a Grecian Urn":—

> "What little Town by river or sea shore
>   Or mountain-built with peaceful citadel
> Is emptied of its folk this pious morn?"

Here he just indicates, glances at the typical smallness of the Greek City-State, the prevailing atmosphere of peacefulness, the prevailing atmosphere of piety. The little town empties itself fearing no plunderers. The little Nation, *en masse*, with singing and dancing and music has gone out into the green woodland to worship the wild God of the wild things and places of the Earth. Everywhere all over Hellas, continental and insular, we find the presence of those minute States in the beautiful dawning of the historic day. Lacedaemonia, for example, used to be called "Hecataupolis" that is the State compounded of a Hundred States; and the learned and judicious Grote thinks that there were even more. But the small States were everywhere.

Returning to our maps—See now South of Attica, between it and the Corinthian territory, the little country of Megara, famous in many ways, chiefly, perhaps, as the parent State of Byzantium; later Constantinople.[42] You will find Megara to be about the size of one of our Irish Baronies. Now, Greek history remembers a time when Megara was divided into 12 kingdoms! They were Clan-communes, doubtless, of which the patriarchs were styled Kings. The little country held 12 such States.

See, too, North of Attica, the famous Baeotian region with its chief City, Classic Thebes, a City second in fame only to Troy in the vast Heroic cycle of the Greeks. Baeotia too was divided amongst a great number of little States and in the centuries when the Demes flourished was occupied by as many Demes proportionally as was Attica. Homer in the Iliad, Book II, enumerates by name 32 such Baeotian States, with respectful and laudatory epithets.

Now, if you compare the maps, you will find that Megara Attica and Baeotia, all together, present an area no greater than our County of Mayo, and much less than our County of Cork. Yet they were held by about one hundred independent States in those centuries of which we know so little, but in which we do know that the genius and virtue of the great Greek race were being mysteriously and divinely fashioned by the Power, however we name it, which guides the destinies of mankind.

There in the silence—for those ages are all but silent to us—there in the darkness—they are dark to us—the Hellenic Man was prepared for his great role as the intellectual lord of mankind.

And every one admits that intellectual lordship of the Greek, but every one does not admit or know that the Greek was the great exponent to mankind of the Art that is the greatest of all, and compared with which that of Pheidias, that of Aeschylus are nothing—the political art.

Aristotle, with the whole Greek world under his very seeing and observing eyes, gives his express approval to the very small Greek States. See Book VII, Chapter IV of his "Politics". He there maintains that a State should be small enough to enable the citizens to be personally acquainted with each other. Otherwise, he adds, they will not legislate wisely and administer the laws justly. Let the number of the citizens exceed that standard, then the City begins to be too great and a Colony should be prepared for. Nature, he says, has predetermined the size of a State as she has predetermined generally the size of all her creatures, trees, fishes, birds, animals, men. She makes men to grow to six feet, or thereabout; does not mean men to be 12 feet high or two feet high. The same law holds for the things that men themselves make. The trireme, for example—it is his illustration—if too big, is unwieldy and ineffective, if too small is only a toy. Nature made man social, and as she has predetermined his individual magnitude, so she has predetermined the size of the Society in which she means him to live. There is a natural size for a Polis, that is a State, a Nation, not indeed rigidly fixed, but varying around a certain standard, and the common-sense philosopher, the School-master of Europe for so many centuries, laid down those common-sense rules for determination of the natural standard.

A Nation—Aristotle would say a Polis—ought to be large enough as to population and territory to maintain itself in comfort and abundance, providing at the same time splendidly for the service of its Gods, and yet small enough to enable the citizens to be acquainted with their fellow citizens, able to understand them and their lives, and sympathize with them. His exact words as to the natural magnitude of States are as follows:

"The first thing necessary, therefore, is that a State should consist of the lowest numbers which will be sufficient to enable the inhabitants to live happily in their political community."[43]

Had the ruling classes of Europe been properly instructed by the teaching classes, by the Universities, they would never have waged such savage, stupid, relentless war, as they have upon all the little European Autonomies, the Village Communes, the Religious Communes, the Guilds and the Boroughs, in their haste to erect huge tyrannical States and vast Empires.

To the great Greek thinker and observer Ireland a Nation would be an absurdity. Ireland, her vast plains and immense sea-board, her far-sundered peoples and territories, governed out of one distant centre of authority, maintained by force would be an Empire, and he had seen enough of Empires and attempted Empires to despise them. The large Tyranny was as detestable to him and to every true Greek as was the small Tyranny. Yet through the irony of Fate he was the tutor of a very great Tyrant indeed—Alexander of Macedon.

And so he also declared, as a primary law of Politics, a law prescribed by Nature herself, that one State ought not to rule over another, that such a relation was contrary to Nature and brought evil to the rulers as well as to the ruled. The Universities of Europe had, for centuries, the exclusive teaching of the aristocracies of Europe. Did they teach them this?

No; the political instruction which they instilled into the tender minds of the young lords and princes of Europe was derived from the brute maxims of old Rome in her dotage, not from the clear wisdom of the Hellene in his prime.

And just observe here—I don't think this has been said before—that the advancing legions of Rome ceased to advance when they reached lands still held by the primitive Aryan clans, the patriarchal Village Communes. Rome was able to conquer countries like Spain, Gaul, and South Britain, countries which had already been self-conquered by emerging native tyrants, and were held in large principalities. She and her legions recoiled before the [typescript missing here].

SIX.

ARCADIA.

Arcadia, like Sparta but for a very different reason, has secured a place of her own in the imagination of mankind. The name has passed into all languages breathing an odour of beautiful pastoral simplicity, naturalness, innocence and happiness. It brings up everywhere thoughts of a kind of felicity and freedom from all care, the dream of which, though the world laughs at it a little, the world, at the same time is unwilling to forego. The word Arcadian will never fail from men's lips however playfully uttered, nor the thing signified from their imaginations and aspirations—not till all the dreams are fulfilled.

Arcadia, situate in the midst of the Peloponesus, and so, quite cut off from the sea, was a land of mountains, glens, and highland valleys, rock, forest, and heather, and of innumerable streams. One of them, by the irony of Fate, a beautiful innocent little stream called the Styx and which never harmed man or beast or plant, has provoked the dread epithet— Stygian, and gone out into all lands and literatures with a very un-Arcadian significance. Above the village of Nonacris in the North East of Arcadia two little white cataracts come tumbling down a steep hillside out of the heather, bright and young and glad. Uniting they roll on to lose themselves after a while, through a chasm, in the cool interior of the earth. That innocent cleft or rift in Arcadian rocks, gave its start to the great chthonian and infernal legend of the Styx. The Nonacrisian children dabble and play in it, and the boys catch trout in it, and laughing Nonacrisian maidens fetch water from it, just as their ancestors did in the days of Epaminondas. And this is the Styx, one of Hell's seven rivers, and dreadful even to the Gods. When the Greek Almighty swore, it was not by himself he swore but by the innocent little stream in which Arcadian boys were catching trout! For imagination, whipped into malignant activity by terror, can play dreadful havoc with the mind of man. And let me here just remark that the thing for which the Styx stands—and that is Death—may, upon experience, be found no more dreadful than that Arcadian stream which frightened Zeus himself.

The Arcadians were always primitive and very little touched at any time by surrounding civilisations. When Pheidias was carving the Olympian Zeus, and Pericles ruling a thousand States out of Athens, when Plato was dreaming in the groves of Academus, and Demosthenes thundering in the Agora, Arcadia was even more primitive than was Attica in the age of the Demes. That is its importance to us. Attica, in the ages when she was divided up into a number of very small States, is prehistoric; Arcadia with its very small States survived and flourished in the full light of history.

The Arcadian Kome or Village-Commune resembled the original Attic Deme. Here the Kome, as there the Deme, was the political and social unit. Arcadia's steams and mountains were not more numerous than her Nations. In the East and South where the land was more level certain strong and war-like City States had indeed emerged. From the lofty summit of Mount Cyllene a man might count at least six shining cities with gates and walls and towers, each with its central strong Acropolis. There was Stymphalus beside its lake, where Hercules with his sharp arrows slew the terrible man-eating winged things, the Stymphalides, the Harpy brood of Lake Stymphalus. It was his sixth labour. He could see Orchomenus, under Mount Erymanthus, where the same hero captured the mighty Erymanthine Boar, the Fifth Labour; warlike Tegea which had more than once defeated the invasive hosts of Sparta herself; Mantinea; Hereum; "windy Enispe" and others; well-walled, strong and proud in the midst of their little territories, owning no masters; every one of them saying, or seeming to say, "I sit a Queen." For these little Cities were independent States, not ruled and not ruling, though they could hear each other's dogs bark and cocks crow. The Mantinean, Tegean, Stymphalian, Orchomenian, knew that between him and all harm was interposed his City with walls 30 feet high, that he had there, and his very own, a noble Temple, a Gymnasium, a Theatre, and an Agora in which every free citizen sat to settle the affairs of State, to listen to his orators, and to govern his government. He came in to his City, perhaps in the dawn, driving his little ass-cart laden with apples, grapes, or vegetables for the market, or with a basket of trout caught in his stream, or driving before him goats or sheep to sell, and clad himself, perhaps, in a goat skin. But at noon he sat in the Agora to listen to his orators and to govern the government, feeling himself a man amongst men, in his own dear country, his own Agora, looked over by his own Gods, in his own beautiful City well secured against the whole world with strong gates and towers and walls 30 feet high. He feared nothing. In wartime if necessary he removed his family and possessions within those strong walls, and waited till the clouds rolled by.

But all the rest of Arcadia, what we may call Arcadia proper, was held by innumerable Village-Communes, mostly Clans, scattered far and wide, little bounded territories with an unwalled Village for their centre; each of them a Deme, independent and self-centred though united with its neighbours by religion and blood and common interests, not drawn together into City-States, not feeling the necessity. Out of such Village-Communes emerged those proud Queens of the East and South. The City of Mantinea, for example, arose from a voluntary drawing together and confederation of five villages. Once it was conquered in war by the Spartans, who razed it to the ground, dispersed the remnant of the broken State into its original five constituent Villages, and enacted there a stern Spartan law governing the new settlement, viz: that no

Village should consist of more than "50 houses" which would represent therefore a population of about 300. The standard or usual Arcadian Village-Commune was therefore of that size. I find too, that the Amphyctionic League, having conquered the Phocians in war, dismantled their Cities and divided the people into Village-Communes of a similar size. The conquerors even fixed the distances which should separate them. It was, I think, two miles. Strong States feared to have Cities on their frontiers; they did not fear Demes. So Spartan State policy was deliberately directed towards the preservation of Arcadia as a land of Villages. Nevertheless, the moment Spartan power declined the five Villages sprang together again and Mantinea re-arose.

Its neighbour, Tegea, consisted of nine constituent Villages. Epaminondas, in the days of Theban supremacy, drew together 40 Arcadian Villages into the new great City of Megalopolis. The Greek Village as distinguished from the Greek City consisted of some 50 houses. That, speaking generally, must have been about the size of those original Attic Demes, out of which grew the 10 Attic States, and, finally, historic Athens.

Behind all the Greek States, Confederations, and petty Empires, we can distinguish many signs of the original Village-Communes.

I maintained that Attica in her Deme stage was a peaceful country, urging amongst other proofs, the fact of her teeming population at that time, and the immense number and prosperity of the Colonies to which she then gave birth.

Now Arcadia, in her corresponding condition, lies in historic light. We can see here in these Arcadian highlands the same striking phenomenon: a land filled with little Deme States of unwalled villages, yet at the same time teeming with population. Contemporary Greek writers often remarked upon the astonishing populousness of this primitive country; also upon the strength, courage, and hardihood of the people. Arcadia was one of the great hives or breeding grounds of Greek Condottieri.[44] It is plain then that those Village-Communes lived together side by side, on the whole peaceably. Savage internal warfare could not have co-existed with such an over-flowing population. The famous "Ten Thousand" were really 15,000; and Xenophon tells us that "half the Greek army consisted of Arcadians and Achaeans." Now the Arcadians and their Captains make a very much more considerable figure in "The Anabasis" than do the Achaeans. They are far more in evidence there, and must have been much more numerous, their country being greater and more famous as a matrix of professional soldiers. We may therefore fairly put down the Arcadian division of Xenophon's famous "Ten Thousand" as at least some 5,000 men.

So, for just one war, in one year, Arcadia sent forth five thousand soldiers of fortune. It is stranger still to learn that such an Arcadia was even prosperous. Xenophon tells us distinctly that the Arcadians in his army were not poor men at all, not men who had been forced abroad for a living. They were scions of rich families, young men who had come out for fun and adventure, hoping to rise in the world and become great and famous. Therefore the total volume of emigration of all classes out of Arcadia, soldiers and labourers, must have been very great indeed.

It is another proof that the little Deme States and Village Autonomies were not at all addicted to fratricidal wars and mutual violence and rapine. Had Arcadia been violence-loving and bloody-minded there would have been no such superfluous population to pour forth. Nor, again, could her name, Arcadia, have gone forth into the general Hellenic mind, breathing that odour of innocence and pastoral simplicity. Nor, once more, would a bloody-minded people have yielded as the Arcadians did, such a large contribution to the vast, heroic, and romantic mythus of the Hellenic race. Pan and Hermes were exclusively Arcadian creations. These Gods did indeed assume new great attributes abroad; but they were primitive enough while at home. Pan was the shepherd God of the Arcadians, the God who took care of their flocks and herds. Hermes was their God of paths and ways. He watched over all travellers, so that evil men feared to injure wayfarers on lonely roads, dreading the vengeance of the road God. His first temple, nay his first image or eloquent symbol, was only a heap of stones by the wayside. But these were everywhere. They served to remind men that the good God Hermes was abroad in the land. And just note here how much true religion saves men in mere expenditure out of pocket. Think of the cost of effectually policing all the lonely roads and mountain paths of Arcadia by the dubious aid of an Arcadian constabulary. The work would have cost near half the revenue of such a country. Now the good God Hermes cost Arcadia nothing; nothing save a little voluntary offering of cakes or milk and wine, and sometimes a kid, cheerfully and gratefully given to him at one of those stony heaps in which he dwelt. Then this invisible policeman was present everywhere, simultaneously on all the lonely roads and ways, and did not grow old or die and require to be replaced. What would be the value of such a policeman to Mexico for example.

If you think of this and extend your reflections you will see how much better off a religious people must always be than an irreligious. Then, as Hermes policed the roads, so Pan the hillsides, defending the flocks and herds, and enabling the shepherd to preserve an easy mind and solace himself with his pipe. Indeed but for Pan and Hermes we would never have heard of Arcadia at all, or only as a hunting ground where men might chase the deer and be themselves chased sometimes by wolves and bears.

Odd as it seems, Pan and Hermes enabled men to live in Arcadia and made and sustained the Arcadian Nation. The Arcadian child lived and moved and had his being in religion. It surrounded him like the atmosphere which he breathed. Nor were authorised trained teachers wanting, men who knew all about that religion and were able to impart it. Many and many a stormy or snowy night when the family group were assembled round the holy Hearth and looked in Hephaistus' glowing friendly face and listened to him as he "laughed" ("Hephaistus is laughing"), a well understood knocking at the door announced to the glad and shouting throng that the divine rhapsodist was at hand. He, the much-longed-for, was here with his grandly rolling hexametres, his inexhaustible store of great delightful tales from the vast wonder-world of the Greek. And the house-mother baked a larger and richer cake for supper, not sparing her cream and eggs, and the house-father drew a greater jug of wine of his best and oldest, and that night there were beating hearts and enlarged eyes as the sacred bard poured forth his treasures. Those great wonder tales are, save the Iliad and Odyssey, now dead. We have only their sorry remnants in "Lempriere,"[45] but they were alive then, told in glowing metric language and brought round to every Greek home by the rhapsodists.

We are not therefore so surprised to learn that when the young Cyrus was advancing into the heart of Asia with his mighty host, the little Arcadian contingent, 5000 or so, compelled the whole army to stop for three days whilst they celebrated games and solemnities in honour of their Pan-Arcadian God, Zeus of Mount Lyceum. The Arcadians would not stir a step till they had rendered his due to their supreme Arcadian God, and the young impetuous Cyrus and his mighty host had to pause and admire. All the Arcadians were children of Zeus, of Zeus and a beautiful Arcadian maiden, Calisto, which means the most beautiful mother, through his divine grace and favour, of the Hero, Arcas, from whom sprang the whole Arcadian race. She was persecuted by a potent enemy against whom Zeus himself could not defend her, some all-but almighty sinister and malignant power. Zeus therefore prepared for her a place in the wilderness, and led her thither, bearing her babe. There he changed her form to that of a bear. As a bear she nursed Arcas in a cave thenceforward holy to all the Arcadian nation. Later, he took her and Arcas to Heaven to himself where they shine for ever, they and their people, in the Northern sky. The Arcadian mother teaching her little children their religion pointed to the glorious constellation of the Bear and told them the story of the divine Father and beautiful lowly Arcadian Mother and the Hero Son. The children knew then why they went in procession once a year to Mount Lyceum, and why they made sacrifices on the altar of Arcas, and why they worshipped someone named Despoina or the Lady.

And you will find in some form the same deep symbolic myth in all these antique religions, and, I suppose, in some form it will last for ever. To the Arcadians it was not a tale or symbol, but a central truth. To every one of Xenophon's Arcadian soldiery it was as sacred as memories of his own Mother and his Home. The modern man smiles at such odd religions. But with her odd religion Arcadia was able to do without a constabulary while it nourished a vast and teeming population.

Would that our own great people, the rulers of the world, could worship the Mother and Child under any form, by any names, in accordance with any tradition. That sinister Mother-and-Child-hating power is out and abroad over the world today pursuing the object of its hatred. If you doubt, go through the great cities.

Now measure this famous Arcadia from side to side; it is about the size of our County of Limerick, but, unlike fertile Limerick, consisted mainly of mountains with intervening highland glens and valleys. Here in the days of Thucydides, of Aristotle and Demosthenes, the Arcadians, producing themselves no famous historians, philosophers, poets, or orators, lived still in that social condition out of which elsewhere the Hellene had emerged to astonish mankind.

As the Greeks of the great Cities became more and more civilised and sophisticated, the more tenderly they regarded Arcadia and things Arcadian. Their feelings towards Arcadia were not unlike those with which a disillusioned man of the world regards fine school boys at play, or merry laughing children at their sports, while he thinks sadly of his own early days. The cultivated Greek had indeed his *Boule*, and *Ecclesia* and *Agora* and great exciting oratory there, also alluring philosophical discussion about Gods, men, and the origin and end of the world, but he felt, in spite of all those privileges, that he had lost something that Arcadia retained. Then his idealised Arcadia got into literature and has been ever since affecting the imagination of the world.

As another example of the power and powerlessness of those small Greek States consider the little island of Naxos. Naxos, besides its fleet, had an army of 8,000 hoplites with their complement of cavalry, and peltasts, and a population of 100,000!—(Grote vol. ii. p. 536). Yet its area was no more than that of an Irish Barony, viz: some 20 miles by 10. Peopled in that proportion an Irish County would exhibit a population of one million and a fighting force of some one hundred thousand men. But indeed all those East Mediterranean countries seem to have been most densely populated. Cast a passing glance here at the Holy Land as it was emerging under the early Kings from its original condition of Clans and Tribes, Village Communes, and very small but strong Cities, remembering that the later Israelites always looked back with a certain regretful tenderness to "the days when there was no King in Israel, when every man did that which was right in his own eyes",[46] though strictly speaking, there never was such a time.

King David's census of the fighting men of Palestine seems to have been carried out very thoroughly, as it is recorded with grave particularity. See ii Samuel Chap. xxiv. Joab and his Captains went through the land in every direction, making lists of the fighting men of Palestine, and at the end of nine months and twenty days handed in the Tale:

"There were in Israel 800,000 valiant men that drew the sword and the men of Judah were 500,000 men."

That is 1,300,000. Besides, there must have been many slaves and men beyond the military age, both of which classes would not have been entered in the lists of "valiant men drawing sword". But if we allow an average of six persons non-military, and old and young, slaves and women, to each unit of the people who drew sword, the population of Palestine in David's time must have been more than nine millions.

If you compare the maps now you will find that you can carve the whole of Palestine out of our one Irish Province of Munster!

Professor Ramsay, who has written so much about Asia Minor, tells us that in his opinion there really was an Age of Gold, that the existence of such an Age was not a mere fancy of the classical poets. He founds his belief upon the number and magnitude of the remains of prehistoric engineering works, of huge reservoirs overlooking now desert lands, aqueducts cut for miles through solid rock, gigantic embankments, etc. etc. He reasons, from this to the presence in remote times of an immense population of mutually friendly and peaceful people, under the control of a religion according to which violence was impious, and labour, especially agricultural labour, a religious duty. In those East Mediterranean lands where the olive was so widely cultivated property must have shed its proverbial timidity, for the man who plants an olive tree must wait for 18 years before he begins to gather the fruit. No wonder that the olive leaf was the symbol of peace and plenty and security from ill. When raging prehistoric Tamerlanes swept over the earth the replanting of the sacred tree was evidence that the deluge had spent itself and the dominion of the robber and slayer at an end for a time.

"And the dove came back to him in the evening, and lo, in her mouth, an olive leaf pluckt off. So Noah knew that the waters had abated from off the earth."[47]

SEVEN.

AN EVENT OF WORLD HISTORY.[48]

One of the greatest events in history occurred silently upon a night in the early summer of 479 B.C., in hollow Lacedæmon, on the banks of the Eurotas, and in the little scattered wide-lying, unwalled City of Sparta. It happened quietly, naturally, like the bursting of a bud or the breaking of a wave.

Envoys from Athens had arrived with an urgent request from the Athenians to the Ephors to dispatch an army into North Greece to defend them against the Persian enemy.

In the previous year, Xerxes, leading back his millions into Asia, had left behind him 300,000 men under Mardonius. In league with him, too, were Macedonia and the whole of North Greece, except Athens, and Mardonius was about to invade Attica.

The envoys were very urgent, passionately eloquent in their entreaty. The five middle-aged Ephors listened impassively. They wore rough home-spun clothing dyed the national colour, a deep red.

"He offered the noblest terms," cried the envoys. "He promised to repair generously all the injuries inflicted upon us by Xerxes in his recent occupation and devastation of our country, promised to extend our territory and to receive us into his friendship and alliance as a Sovereign equal and independent Power."

Though unable to make resistance, we replied that "so long as the Sun held his course in the Heavens we would not desert the cause of the Greeks."

The middle-aged men demanded time for consideration: three days. It was a grave request. Sparta did nothing without due deliberation. On the fourth they required three days more: it was a very grave request. Sparta had never before put forth her strength beyond the Isthmus.

On the eighth they had not yet reached agreement. The patience of the passionate Athenians was worn out.

"If you do not give us a reply to-morrow at the rising of the sun we leave Sparta on the instant, and we shall counsel our countrymen to make terms with the foreigner."

They withdrew, raging, to their quarters. That day, far and wide, there was a certain movement, motion: the Spartan Empire was astir. That night there marched through and out of Sparta into the North 5,000 Spartans and 35,000 Helots—for war purposes as good as the Spartans, trained in their drill—and 10,000 Periœci, free men of famous Achæan stock, and the best men upon the Globe, perfect at the drill and weapons, and to whom, Helots and Periœci and Spartans alike, it was unlawful to leave the battlefield alive: contrary to the Law and therefore unthinkable.

The Athenians did not see them or hear them as they passed.

"Not hear?"

No. The sixty thousand went silently, like lightning. There was no sound of trampling from those 120,000 feet. Shoeless and sandalless were these antique braves, so trained as men and boys and children. It was one of their few laws.

The Moon was at the full: Sparta could only act then! They passed in enomoties of twenty-five, eight a-breast, and the enomotarch: corselets, shields, helmets, the rows of long, sloping spears—enomoty after enomoty without end: a living torrent of drilled human valour, but unlike a torrent, silent: not a sound.

And the Sun rose, and the Athenians pale and determined, as silent and grave now as any Laconian man, hastened to the Ephoralty, and demanded an immediate answer to their ultimatum.

"We sent the army," replied the Ephors. "It marched in the night, and is already over the Arcadian frontier."

"Its strength?" enquired the delighted Athenians, near weeping with joy.

"Sixty thousand," replied the crimson-clad, "having the due complement of peltasts (archers and slingers). There are more to follow.

The well-informed and intelligent Athenians were dumb-founded. Never before had such a force, or half or a third of such force, been put forth on Greek soil. The strength of Sparta was unknown: it was known now. The veiled war-power stood unveiled, ready to act, and acting; on the instant.

Sparta had been slow, seemingly, sluggish, inert, and apathetic ever since these Persian troubles began: motionless, like a boulder stone on a mountain side, like a cloud resting quietly and as if for ever on one of the peaks of her own Taygetus. Then the hour arrived, and the moment, and the word of command from the Ephoralty, and Sparta went—like a thunderbolt.

The issue of the war for Mardonius and his 300,000 Persians was at that moment as sure as the fate of a heron held in chase by an eagle. The fate of Mardonius was sealed.

"You speak of the Spartan Empire. The phrase is new to me. What was its extent?"

About the size of our County of Mayo.

"But it must have had vast wealth derived from commerce and manufacturing industries to support such a power."

No. Not a seaport. No exports or imports at all.

"You speak of their Laws as if known and familiar to all. I suppose they were written out and the MSS. studied in the schools."

No. They were not written at all. They were alive, in men's hearts. No one in the Empire was able to read or write. The Ephors may have had a slave as their foreign secretary; I don't think they had.

"Then the Spartans were uneducated?"

Yes; all illiterates. They would have been excluded from our polling booths, and from Australia. There was not a Primary School amongst them, or an Intermediate, or a University. And the mothers of the 60,000 had been, as girls, brought up in a similar state of ignorance.

"I think you cannot be serious."

I am.

"You surprise me speaking as you do about the Helots. I thought they were a poor wretched lot of down-trodden serfs, made to get drunk as educational object lessons, and so forth."

So did I.

"Their Helots, too, you say would not leave a battlefield alive."

Yes. Consider this. Every one knows about Leonidas and his 300. It is not generally known that around Leonidas at Thermopylæ there perished not only the 300 Spartans but also 3,000 Spartan Helots! Xerxes counted the slain, found them 4,000. There were 300 Spartans, 750 Thespians, a few Thebans: the rest, 3,000, were Helots.

"If what you say is correct History would seem to be a kind of liar."

A snob rather. Carlyle calls her "a poor slut".[49]

"The Spartans seem to have been a singular people."

Very, and not in any one thing but in a series of things.

You are probably not aware that, if a Spartan officer of State summoned to him the greatest citizen of the little Empire, the greatest citizen did not walk smartly in obedience to the summons.

He ran.

So I have seen men-of-war; men run to the call of an officer with a cheery "Ay, Ay Sir."

What discipline!

Yes. A very singular people. And I'm sure you are not aware of this—that they were the only people of the ancient-world who kept no slaves.

What?

Yes, no slaves. The Helots could not be bought and sold or treated in any way as chattel and personal property. The State alone owned them and stood between them and the Lords of the lands in which they worked. They were *adscripti glebæ*[50] not chattel property of any one. And their rents as such were fixed by Spartan law and unalterable. To the lords of land they paid half the corn wine and oil which their holdings produced.

Now, the Athenians who have left us so many lively stories about the Spartans and their Helots used to exact from their own free tenants five sixths of the produce of the lands of Attica. You will find both these facts in Bury's History of Greece.[51] In Athens or Attica things were largely governed by competition, personal love of gain, and "deil take the hind-most."[52] Not so in Sparta where the competition was all about honour and virtue and the good of the State and where the laws, including this as to rent, were made for permanency and had, or for long centuries seemed to have, the stability of Parnon and Taygetus and the certainty of the flow of the Eurotas, that well-rolling river.

Would you like to hear a little about the origin of these Spartans, the race from whose loins they sprang?

Assuredly.

EIGHT.

THE SILENT RACE.[53]

When Byron was brooding over the possibility of an insurgent and re-surgent Greece, he thought especially of the Dorians, whether any true Dorian blood still ran there to answer the call of the captains, and thought there did.

> "On Suli's steep and Parga's shore
> Exists the remnant of a line
> Such as the Doric mothers bore:
>   And here perhaps some seed is sown
>   The Heracleidan blood might own."[54]

"Heracleidan," for the Doric-Spartan Chiefs claimed descent from Heracles.

When Milton saw the Satanic hosts pass in review under the eyes of their dread commander, their visages and stature as of gods, their order and discipline, their intricate rhythmic martial combinations and separations, and felt in every sympathetic nerve the presence there of death-defying courage, of silent resolved loyalty and bravery, he, too, thought of Dorians:

> "Anon they move
> In perfect phalanx to the Dorian mood
> Of flutes and soft recorders."[55]

Who were the Dorians?

A little to the north of Delphi on the map of North Greece you will find a small, vacant white spot, showing clear in the midst of the darkly-marked surrounding mountains. There a bowl-shaped hollow in the hills supplies the husbandman with a field for his labour. It is an alluvial valley and plain, good for corn and kine, for the apple and vine, the olive and the fig, a green land fit for the sustenance of man and beast, and traversed by many streams and rivulets descending from the hills which gird it round upon all sides. That little valley was the cradle and nursery of one of the world's great races, the mountain eyrie of an eagle brood.

At some time far beyond the reach of history, a little Greek Clan who called themselves Children of Dorus—and so the Dorians—in one way or another got possession of the valley and called it after their own name, Doris. Like all the Greeks, they seem to have come down out of the north-west, from Illyria. They established friendly relations with the neighbouring Hellenes, with the Phocians, the Aetolians, the Ozolian and Opuntian Locrians, especially with the sacred families who held and administered holy Delphi where Apollo dwelt and gave oracles, chief counsellor and adviser of all the Hellenes in his time. He was especially dear to the Dorians. Their ancestor, Dorus, was his son.

In that little plain in the hills the Dorians lived, throve, and multiplied, utterly ignored by the great Hellenic world outside, known only, but creditably known, to their own neighbours. The civilised Greek world knew nothing about them. Homer, who has celebrated those more ancient neighbouring nations, was quite ignorant of the strong, quiet little nation that dwelt here, hidden from all eyes, like a child unborn. Here, nevertheless, was generated, conceived, and grew to birth, adolescence and maturity, one of the greatest of Earth's human races, that one, too, which, strangely enough, had the least to say about itself. But for their deeds and but for that rare gift of speech which was enjoyed by other Greek races we would to-day know nothing at all about the Dorians. That bowl-shaped depression in the hills above Delphi, the cradle and nursery of the Dorians, was no greater as to area than an Irish barony or English hundred. A man might stroll across the Dorian territory from boundary to boundary between sunrise and noon in a leisurely manner, pausing often to observe the mountain scenery, the vine plantations and corn-fields, and to converse with the people, responding not too copiously in their clear, pure Doric Greek. But in this small space a great people were being fashioned by destiny, and carefully guarded there in that remote fastness from the influences which were elsewhere corrupting and destroying Hellenic peoples once as noble as themselves. I do not believe that the little original Clan coming down hither out of Illyria, with their mules and donkeys carrying their small possessions, fought their way. I believe that they bought it. Brave as any, the insane war passion was never strong in any of the Hellenes. All we know is that the Dorians came and made their home there, and that no one was able, or even perhaps willing, to make them go away. The little Clan soon threw out sub-clans, branches of the parent stock, till the valley all over was dotted with villages, patriarchal small states of the primitive village-commune type, united like one family in a bond of common blood and traditions, inter-alliances by marriage, friendly mutual services, and the enthusiastic common worship of Apollo, who, unseen, was always in their midst.

Then out of these scattered villages of the tribe, according to an instinct common to all the Greek race, there emerged four city states; four or six villages combining to create a city with a great satisfying civic life not attainable through villages. But the four Dorian cities were friends, though each had its own distinct life, four queens, but also four sisters, hence the historic Dorian Tetrapolis, the four-citied state of Doris. These city states were Pindus, Erineum, Cytinium, and Borium.

Favoured by God and Man the Dorians multiplied and prospered, till the time came when they felt an oppressive need of expansion, that the time had come for the bursting of these mountain barriers, the sending forth of a new nation. The Dorian hive swarmed.

All the wild surrounding regions, held too by friendly neighbours who regarded them with affection and respect,

perhaps with awe, did not supply a country fit for settlement.
There were two ways by which they might break forth into
the outer world; one northwards through the country of the
Opuntian Locrians to the Ambracian Gulf, and thence to the
Thracian coast, the Hellespont and Black Sea. The other lay
southward through the country of the Ozolian Locrians to the
Corinthian Gulf, where the Mediterranean lay before them.
They chose this last way. But the Dorians, sheer inlanders as
they were, ploughmen and vine-dressers and shepherds, knew
nothing of the sea. They had no ships, and did not know how
to build them. But that was nothing: Greek lads, the quickest,
most intelligent and versatile of mankind, could rapidly learn
to do or to make anything in reason, and the Dorians were as
Greek as any.

Dorian lads crossed the hills, came down to the port of
Naupactus (it means the place of the making of ships), and
there from older and wiser men, the native Naupactian ship
carpenters, soon learned how to build ships—big transport
ships, and long, swift brazen-beaked, deadly-looking war
ships, penteconters with twenty-five oars on each side. The
trireme, with her three banks of oars on each side, had not yet
been invented. There the young Dorians learned rapidly how
to build ships, and row them and sail them, and the whole art
of marine navigation as well, till the inland agricultural and
pastoral Dorians became as familiar with the Sea as with the
Earth, and exchanged the lowing of kine and the bleating of
sheep for the roaring of waves and the howling of storms.
Soon the Dorian mountaineers became the most daring,
experienced, and far-travelling of all seafaring nations.

You, young men and lads of my own time, who intend
to play a brave part and to be yourselves the founders of
nations, do not forget the lesson of Naupactus and the
Dorian boys learning seamanship there. When you have well
founded your inland food-producing industrial commonwealth
let the first colony, or one of the first, be planted by you upon
the seaboard, and establish there your own Naupactus, well
supplied by you of the interior with food, timber, tools, raw

materials, and everything that a stirring Irish Naupactus might require.

Meantime at home, the Dorian Boulé, the Chiefs of the Nation, having consulted deeply with travelled men and sailor-merchants, decided upon Elis in the Peloponesus as the site of the first settlement. They sent ambassadors thither and arranged terms with the Eleans. The great Hellenic expansions, the Æolian, the Ionian, and now the Dorian, were, upon the whole, peaceful, conducted everywhere mainly by treaty, presents, exchanges, and contracts.

When all was settled and the sanction of the God at Delphi obtained, the new nation, perfectly organised from the start, equipped already as a Sovereign State, lacking only land, with hearts glad yet sad, left the little valley and climbed the mountain passes leading toward Naupactus.

I call attention to a religious feature of the emigrant procession, not this time to the sacred fire which was there, too, taken from the ever-burning National Dorian fire of the Tetrapolis, but to something else of a religious nature not so easily understood in our time. At the head of the bright, many-hued column which wound its way through the brown mountain passes, was borne on high an upright severed section of a tree trunk, always in the van. It was upheld upon a frame through which long poles passed and the whole rude structure carried upon men's shoulders. There were no roads here, only footpaths and mule tracks. Before it and behind went youths and maidens singing joyfully and playing upon flutes and three-stringed lyres.

What was this wooden upright pillar, borne so carefully and besung so loudly and gladly? It was the God of the young Nation. The young Dorian Nation was going forth into the wide, wide world, but not by themselves, not unbefriended or uncared for. Apollo himself was going with them. He was in their van and at their head. The wooden pillar was Apollo.

Very strange, indeed, and to us all but incredible. Nevertheless, all such primitive peoples, so taught, as it would seem by Nature herself, had some such way of symbolising for themselves things that they could not express in words. It was so universally. The religions of Europe to-day, however, august and superior to rude symbolism, had an humbler original than men suspect.

See Gen., c. 28, v. 22, the story of the sacred pillar stone at Bethel: "And this stone shall be the house of the Lord"; that is, the Lord's dwelling place. Also, Joshua, c. 24, v. 27, where Joshua speaks of a similar pillar stone as hearing and bearing witness.

Young Ætolia joined the Dorians in that first Peloponesian settlement. It resulted eventually in the Ætolo-Dorian absorption of Elis, the creation there of a new people soon to become famous over the whole world as the guardians and presidents of the great Pan-Hellenic Olympian festivals of Supreme Zeus.

The greatest human-divine figure ever carved by the hand of man was the Statue of Zeus at Olympia. It was the work of Pheidias, made by him to the order of the descendants of the men who came up out of that little mountain valley bearing before them that shapeless an-iconic pillar, and hymning their bit of timber, calling it Apollo, God, Father and Friend.

But the people who worshipped the bit of oak or ash or pine, calling it their Father, Friend, Captain and Protector, singing loud and clear their choral songs, were better, braver, purer and nobler by far, by very far, than the highly civilised, cultured and cultivated people who, in the great temple of Olympian Zeus on the banks of the Alpheus, worshipped, or thought they worshipped, the august, unsurpassed figure carved by Pheidias to be the wonder of the whole world.

The Dorian hive, as I said, swarmed; also it kept swarming. The native virtue, vitality of the race, continually re-created the oppressive sense of numbers and periodically impressed on the Dorian mind the necessity of expansion. And so generation after generation, and century after century, the Dorian swarms took wing up through those mountain passes and down into Naupactus out of that miraculous teeming hive in the hills above Delphi, down and out over the Corinthian Gulf, southwards, always southwards, gradually taking possession of, annexing, absorbing, Dorizing every country in which they settled. They were not so civilised, so cultured, so clever, perhaps, as were the other contemporaneous Greek races, but they had in them, more than all the rest, something which, for want of a better name, we may perhaps call character.

The Dorians remind one much of a somewhat kindred modern race, the Normans. The Normans starting from a little territory in the north of Norway, under Rollo the Ganger, spread themselves far and wide over Europe, annexing and Normanising many lands by virtue too, I think, mainly of Character. They were simpler, braver, sincerer, in a word, more downright honest, I believe, than their contemporaries.

After Elis the stream of Dorian emigration aimed towards the fertile plains of Messenia, the next Peloponesian land to the South, pouring in there through "Sandy Pylos," so celebrated as the home of old Nestor in the heroic ages. Here, now, the young northern nation kept continually arriving, steadily absorbing, Dorizing all the old Achæan clans there.

From Messenia pioneer scions of the race made their way up the passes of Taygetus, got down into Laconia, settled there on the banks of the Eurotas, and emerged into History as the ever memorable Spartans or Lacedemonians.

Other swarms passed round the Peloponesus in ships, entered and took possession of Argos and the Argolid, took possession of Corinth, of Megara, of Ægina, of Salamis on the Attic Coast.

They went to Crete and made Crete half Dorian.

All the rest of the coast of Asia Minor being already colonised from Greece they aimed for the South and colonised there the Carian, Lycian and Pamphylian coasts and the adjacent isles. Pamphylia is a Dorian name.

Then, remember that out of all these various countries the Dorian City-States there began soon themselves to organise and send forth equipped new nations, of their own, founding new City-States far and wide over the Mediterranean from Sardinia to the Black Sea and the Sea of Azof, hundreds of them, nor would it be an exaggeration, I think, to say thou-

sands, great and small, and, as we know, a Greek State could
be very small indeed. For example, near twenty Cities were
daughters of Corcyra, which was a daughter of Corinth,
which was a daughter of the little far-off ancient mother in
the hills above Delphi. Some of these Dorian daughters of
daughters became very powerful and illustrious, Byzantium,
Tarentum, Naples, Syracuse.

Now, having looked well at all these great, extensive,
famous regions annexed, absorbed by this astonishing people,
turn back again and consider the little blank spot above
Delphi in the midst of the darkly-marked mountains, the little
Dorian Tetrapolis across whose territory a man might stroll in
leisurely fashion between breakfast and lunch.

Looking myself again at it and at the countries of the great
and famous nations which derived from it, a quaint thought
occurs to me. Sometimes, in the course of my life, I have seen,
and perhaps you have, a frail, slight, sweet-faced, white-haired
old lady in the midst of her tall daughters and gigantic sons,
all fond of her, playing with and petting her. Here, too, in our
map we see the little ancient genetrix of a giant brood. And
this brood of great nations too was ever loyal to the little
genetrix. Presents and gifts and kind messages were sent to
little Doris from afar by her far-scattered children, and when
they, too, in their day time equipped and sent forth new
nations they derived their captains of the same, Œkists as they
called them, from the old home in the Locrian mountains. On
each occasion the little ancient Tetropolis supplied the Œkists.
Then at last the little mother failed and faded. The Dorian
Tetropolis remained, known to historians and geographers, but
Doris had fulfilled her destiny. The little mother had borne,
nursed, educated, and sent out into the world her great children. But when Doris was in her youth and prime was there
a country then on the earth's surface which could be compared with her? No. Not Babylonia, in spite of her hanging
gardens, her towering walls, Chaldee armies, her subject states;
not Assyria, her cruel devastative kings; not Egypt. The greatest
spot on the earth was little Doris, hid away folded from harm

in the embrace of the Locrian mountains. Little Doris and her God were going to beat them all.

If it were my good fortune to be able to visit Greece I would go first, not to the sad graveyards of the dead civilisations, but to that hidden valley with its ramparts of ever-during hills, ever-springing greenery, ever-living fresh waters, where the heroic little mother raised her great children, with everything all round still fresh and pure and living, and with holy nature, the ever young, still queen and mistress of all. To-day, perhaps, in some such quiet spot, making no noise at all in the newspapers, the good angel of mankind may be preparing some such people to be the saviours of the World, free, as the Dorians were not, from the little unnoticed seeds of crime and insanity which, in their germination, first maddened and then destroyed that great race and all the Hellenes.

The Greeks loved liberty more than any other people in history, and hated war more than any other people. They loved beauty so much that they almost made both beautiful; but, in the end, the crimes which they had tolerated destroyed them.

NINE.

HOMER'S MEN.

Historians are in agreement as to some such gradual peaceful infiltration of the Hellene into Greece; for the earliest historic Greeks retained no memory or tradition at all of an age of violent invasion and unsettlement. The Hellenes kept trickling into and through all continental Greece gradually but completely Hellenising the original inhabitants who so incorporated them, their manners, Gods, and civilisation, adopting also their beautiful, vital, unsurpassed language, that in the end they forgot utterly that they ever had been anything else than true Hellenes since the dawn of time.

Homer's heroes, nevertheless, assuredly represent a race of essential warriors of the North European type. They are the same kind of men whom we meet in the Irish bardic heroic literature. I note the same immense personal pride, the same stately courtesy amongst themselves within their own order, the same chastity of their women, graciousness, and beautiful manners, the same genuine hospitality, frankness and boldness; resemblances many. Then this is most noteworthy. The Homeric heroes disappeared, vanished utterly, in Hellas. The great Greeks of the historic age were altogether unlike the Homeric. They were essentially civic men and patriots. Solon and Pericles, Lycurgus, Brasidas, Gylippus, Epaminondas, Aratus of Sicyon, all the great historic Greeks lost themselves, became great by losing themselves, in the cause of their Polis, of their country and fellow-citizens. Had Homer's heroes been invited to submerge their grand individualities in any such absurd aggregate of common people including fellows like Conon! and Thersites! they would simply not have understood; and if they did understand the resulting language would have been awful, the beautiful hexametre would have fled affrighted before it. They could never tame themselves to the aggregate life of the Polis; and so, as the Polis arose, fed and sustained by the universal love and devotion, by the genius and morale of the whole Greek race, those astonishing Homeric men had to go: there was no room for them in the Polis; and, shame of shames! as they went, they could hear Thersites bawling in the Agora, well and strong and in good voice. They were quite unfit for civil life, but they were grand human types nevertheless, and while Man is on the earth he will turn and return to contemplate them with a curious mixture of sympathy and awe. We seem to know better, to have more in common with them than with the great historic Greeks. Good or bad they were so made as to be incapable of being anything but their own sheer selves. They would not, could not, stunt themselves, stint themselves in speech or action to meet any external standard of propriety. They said what they felt and did what they liked. The wide-ruling Agamemnon, King of men, declared to a crowd of his peers that his slave girl, Chryseis, was much preferred by him to his lawful spouse, that she was superior to her in beauty and in mind and in needlework. It was not a gentlemanly speech, but he felt in that way, and said what he felt.

Later, when tribulation came upon him, his groanings resembled the thunder of Zeus when out of a black cloud charged with snow he thunders mightily. To the groaning succeeded a moaning which the poet compares with the roar of a crowded city. The fact that the whole of the Grecian camp was listening to the noise did not restrain him.

"Die, dog!" cries Achilles to the noble vanquished Hector. "I have in my mind to eat your very flesh raw."

He was true to type then, to his own uncontrollable wild self, just as much as when he sang sweetly to the accompaniment of his phorminx, or treated Agamemnon's mighty eric as a kind of filth, or wept, thinking of his dear father far away, or received honoured visitors in his tent with hospitable joy and the most delicate courtesy.

Elsewhere Achilles was a God, God of the Euxine, Achilles Pontarchus. Indeed all the Homeric heroes seem to have been local Greek deities swept here together into the great Epic and compelled to figure there as mortal demi-gods. And I believe that Homer never forgot the marine source of Achilles, and so invested his character with something of the terrible insensate savagery as well as the mysterious beauty of the Sea. He made him at the same time the most shockingly cruel of the Greeks, and the most beautiful.

All Homer's heroes had this attribute of unmastered self-will, of unmeasured pride in themselves. Nor did they think the very Gods so much their superiors. They can bring indignant charges against Zeus himself. Diomede wounds and puts Ares to flight and roars insults after the retreating God.

We have all an immense pride which we are afraid and ashamed to display. We have all a deep conviction that we have an absolute and unconditional right to do what we please, to do and to say just what we like, to be as free as the winds and the waves; and no laws or religions will ever beat that conviction out of man's heart, that he was meant to be free and amenable to no law whatsoever but his own, subject to no other will or any power of congregated and assenting wills but only to his own will.

All great individual types of character, even the criminal, such as Napoleon, arrest, hold, and fascinate the imagination, for the same reason. In some way or other they suggest, indicate, that absolute freedom and uncontrolled self-will, pride in self, confidence in self, which men feel to be their native right, a birthright which they lack the courage to claim, which, through their weakness, they have abnegated. It is a Satanic spirit perhaps, but it exists, and it exists for reasons. What else but this, or something like this, which words cannot express, has lifted up Man from a mere nothing, a speck, an atom, to be what he is, the indubitable terrible Lord of this Planet?

Homer is the greatest mind that ever expressed itself in literature, and it is a world-wonder greater than any other, the appearance of such a spirit at such a time. How he notes all things, simple, natural, beautiful: the infant on its mother's breast, small and beautiful like a star, the little girl child whimpering, holding on to its mother's skirt, crying to be taken up; the little boy building castles on the sands of the sea; the patient oxen in the furrow; the fall of the patriarchal tree in the forest; the fascinating behaviour of the wild fierce creatures there. But enough. It is too late in the day to begin praising Homer. I note that he helped to laugh away the Aeolian Pantheon. And yet he made exceptions. Hermes is always good and beautiful, the Raphael of the Greeks, the faithful road-God, the conductor. Apollo is always great and noble, essentially divine. The Iliad begins with his moving in his wrath down Olympus "like night": almost the first sound there is the dread clang of his silver bow, and we are left at the end thinking perhaps more about him than about Achilles. We know that he is just about to kill the terrible and horrible Peleides.

My theme, however, is the wonderful Greek Polis, not the wonderful Greek God. Yet note here that, for the Greek, Apollo was the founder of those thousands of Greek cities, not one of which was built without the express sanction of the God.

More than that, a Greek poet, Callimachus, wrote this strange line concerning him:

"He loves the founding of Cities. With his own hands he lays the foundation stones."

The oecist in performing that sacred act became for the moment Apollo himself. When Faith is strong men seem able to believe almost anything.

The Greek Polis was no mere collection of houses in which men lived. The Gods were fellow citizens living there too in their temples and receiving their share of all good things. Their names were inscribed in the lists of the citizens.

Homer was not made in the little island of Chios or by the Aeolian Greeks of Asia or by those pre-historic war lords whom he celebrates. He was the product of a great and gifted race which for unknown, unrecorded millenniums, had been generating that which at last took form in him.

"Happy the nations that have no history." This is not a paradox but a fact.

The Aeolian Greeks had no history, yet they produced—Homer! The Ionian Greeks had no history, yet they produced—Athens! The Dorian Greeks had no history, yet they produced—Sparta! Homer and Athens and Sparta were prepared in the womb of an immense past of which we know nothing, about which we can only make dim and uncertain conjectures as we consider the huge Greek national mythus and the exquisite vital Greek language.

That while they were in the main innocent, virtuous, and pious, is proved not only by the marvellous creations to which they subsequently gave birth, but by their peaceful pre-historic Hellenisation of Greece, and then by their fecundity and multiplication, and the consequent Hellenic expansion over seas, that profuse scattering of Greek cities like a spray all over the shores of the Mediterranean and the Euxine.

As the Greeks emerge into history we perceive the beginning of the great decline, the noble Greek descending to a state in which the fierce ignorant, but earnest, Jew could honestly scorn the violet-crowned Athens, and the stern Roman sincerely despise the *Graeculus esuriens*.[56] I am touching the most serious question with which the mind of man can concern itself, the causes of the corruption of noble peoples, of the depravity which follows civilisations like their shadow, of the nature of what we call evil. Why is history such a calendar of crime and insanity? Why, in this Paradise of a World, is Man such a blot on the fair force of creation?

"Happy the nations that have no history."

It is no paradox, but as true as any such condensed and concentrated statement can well be.

It is a law which is always in operation. Lead a life innocent and virtuous and these daily organs of fame which collect the materials of history take no notice of you. Commit one crime and they will celebrate you. Commit a great crime and you may be in history. Thousands of millions of Greek men loved and honoured their Gods and uttered humble prayers in their temples, and lived and died leaving nothing to be gathered by the gleaning historians. Foolish Eratosthenes burned the great temple of Diana of the Ephesians. He is in history.

Small rascals have been many in Ireland. Ralph Sadlier[57] cheated thousands of their money, and was found one sunny morning in a grassy ditch self-slaughtered, a silver cup by his side. He is historical.

Cheat, grind, grasp, become rich, and the newspapers bow down before you and history looks enquiringly in your direction. Murder on a great scale and you are sure of a niche in her temple. The old Assyrian kings are there. They, as regularly as the coming of the Spring, went forth out of Nineveh to rob mankind and desolate the world, to crush young noble nationalities like that to which we owe the Old Testament. Yet as men they were only criminal degenerates from the primitive virtuous old Semitic farmers of the Tigris valley from whom they sprang, and about whom history is silent. She is loud about the criminalities and insanities of imperial Rome, silent about the Ramnes Tities and Luceres,[58] dumb about the times when the grand Roman character was being formed, eloquent about its corruption.

And, most assuredly, the great English character was never formed in these late centuries of commercialism and Empire. Rather, England is today living upon and consuming something accumulated in times prehistoric or extra-historic, just as Greece in those blazing centuries of her glory, the fifth and fourth B.C., used up, dissipated, squandered, a wealth of human power and virtue which had been slowly accumulating through millenniums of which history knows nothing.

The Asian-Greek Aeolian civilisations, out of which Homer sprang, is pre-historic. All those Kings and Chiefs, Demi-gods and Gods who live and move in his poems, are pre-historic. His Kings, themselves pre-historic, only traditionally remembered, had emerged as war-lords, territorial captains, out of Greek peoples having an ancient and ancestral civilisation of their own, and who dwelt by clans and families and aggregations of the same in unwalled villages and little walled towns. And we know nothing at all about them; they are all pre-historic, just as pre-historic as the contemporaneous village communes of the Danube valley and of all North Europe. They, too, did not begin to be historic until they began to be conquerors, to rob, slay, and exploit upon a great scale. From universal history take away art and literature and religion, and what remains is concerned mainly with conquest and Empire, that is with exploitation, rapine, and slaughter. Like all the other Greeks, the Aeolians too advanced, sowing Cities. In their first wave of expansion they scattered a crowd of Aeolian cities over North Asia Minor and the adjoining islands, chief of them Troy. We are apt to forget that the Trojans were true Greeks; their manners and customs, their language and their Gods were all Greek, Hellenic. As to the crowd of Aeolian Cities—Achilles boasts that he alone, he with his Myrmidons, had stormed and sacked twelve marine cities and eleven inland.

In later historic times we find an Aeolian federation of 12 cities in the valley of the Hermus, and those 12 giving birth to 30 more in the region of the Scamander and Mount Ida, and a great though unknown number in other directions. Wherever they came and wherever they went the Aeolian Greeks, like the Dorians and the Ionians, scattered abroad little City-States, proud, self-sufficing, self-reliant, sovereign Nations; ready for war if necessary; every citizen a soldier and rower in the war-triremes; but hating war nevertheless, and loving above all other things the cult of their Gods and religious solemnities, festivities, processions, and dramatic religious representations in their honour.

The Greeks are the grand champions and representatives in history of the idea of the small State and its realisation in practice. Historians ascribe the cause of that phenomenon to the multitude of the mountain ranges which divided Greece

into small valleys and exiguous plains. But that is no expla-
nation. Boeotia was permeable enough to armies, yet there
were 12 Boeotian States.

Aristotle, having under his observation hundreds of States
of all kinds, from little clan Communes and Village Republics
to small Empires, declared it to be the intention of Nature
herself that men should live in communities sufficiently great
in population and territory to maintain a dignified and happy
life, and yet small enough to enable the citizens to know and
sympathise with each other. Therefore, he argued, all imperialism, all government by force of one City by another City, is
contrary to Nature.

A word about this unimpassioned phrase—"Contrary to
Nature". Socrates was still sufficiently under the control of the
ancestral Greek religion to think of good as that which was
in harmony with the will of the Gods, and as evil everything which was opposed to that will. But Aristotle and the
other successors of Socrates, all somewhat dubious about the
Greek Pantheon, spoke of good as that which is contrary to
Nature.

The Greek self-restraint in the use of language must not
hide from us the weight of moral disapprobation with which
those men regarded conduct which they only spoke of as
"contrary to Nature".

Aristotle, having before him the criminal and tragical career
of imperial Athens, her attempted exploitation of a thousand
weaker City-States, declared imperialism to be contrary to
Nature, and the old Greek self-sufficing Polis to be the natural
form of human society. It was that kind of social State in
which Nature meant Man to live, the human aggregation
which was most favourable to the attainment of the highest
kind of felicity, virtue and prosperity.

He was followed in this respect by Plato whose ideal Polis,
generally called "Plato's Republic", was a self-sustained, self-
sufficing community aiming towards the realisation of the
highest good and therefore determined against Imperialism,
because the conquest and exploitation of other States was

bound to work internal confusion and destroy its inner harmony, integrity and unity.

Now it is very interesting to find that only a little before the time of Plato and Aristotle, that is about 500 B.C., the greatest of Chinese philosophers, Lao-Tse, was in China declaring the same law.

"My political ideal," he wrote, "is a nation composed of a great number of independent villages. These villages will hear each other's dogs bark and cocks crow, and will not desire to have any nearer relations."

The truth here is expressed with that kind of violence that we find in all proverbs. Lao-Tse had not the Greek love of full and exact statement. That is an Aryan necessity or propensity not felt by the Asiatic. But Lao-Tse meant exactly the same thing as Aristotle. That is to say, Nature which has made Man at the same time intensely social and exceedingly weak and dependent, meant him to live in societies of a certain magnitude, and meant these societies to be so happily absorbed in their own interests and occupations that they would not care to assume the labour and anxiety and also the great and evident peril of trying to govern similar neighbouring societies, much less the bloody work of conquering and exploiting them with the equal chance of being themselves conquered and exploited.

It is near two thousand five hundred years since the excellent Lao-Tse delivered himself of that bit of philosophy, and since then what countless thousands of millions of Chinese people have lived and died consciously or unconsciously practising in a very considerable degree, Lao-Tse's recommendation which was in fact no more than this:—

"Live naturally, rightly, kindly, and pleasantly with your friends and relations, and don't bother about other people whom you don't know. Leave them alone."

And indeed wherever Nature's quiet voice can be heard men are inclined to think in this way and live in this way. He called his philosophy Tao (the Way), and declared that the Tao was old, very old, and had been understood and practised by millions before his time. The wise, he said, had been always Taoists.

That wild young conquering hero Pyrrhus of Epirus, from whom we derive the convenient phrase, "a Pyrrhic victory", had a philosopher friend called Cineas, to whom at the beginning of his career, he confided his ambitions whose range was sufficiently great and spacious.

"I shall make myself lord of Epirus to begin with," he said. "I shall then bring Macedonia and all Greece under my dominion."

"And after that?" enquired the Sage.

"I shall then hurl all this combined power upon Asia and play again the glorious role of the great Alexander."

"And then?"

"Then I shall turn my attention to the West, take possession of the Carthaginian Empire and of as much of Italy as is worth conquering."

"And after that?"

"After that," said the youth, "after that I shall probably rest and enjoy myself."

"And why not do that now?" replied Cineas. "You have hereditary estates, wealth in abundance, fine hunting grounds in the Molossian Hills, all the ways and means of enjoyment including health and strength and youth. Why draw upon yourself such vast labours and sufferings in order to do as a tired old man, perhaps lacking a leg, what you can do now as a young, and with both your legs in good health?"

This is just what Lao-Tse would have said to that ambitious youth, and what, doubtless, Aristotle often said to his distinguished pupil, Alexander of Macedon, and equally in vain. For a man might as well preach to a torrent to go quietly as to young ambition to alter its thoughts. For the fact is, I may as well say it here, that the Tao is only half the truth and that Man is born a warrior, but that the war to which he is born is a divine war, not an infernal. Then his thinkers and teachers must let him loose there. Once shown the way and the goal of it and let loose there he will go like a—hurricane, and as uncontrollably.

Meantime, note that it is people like Lao-Tse who keep the world together in spite of all the hustlers. If there were no quiet people to check them, these last, the hustlers, would very soon between them rend the world to fragments and clear the race of men off the Planet. And is it not deeply interesting to find the two greatest and most famous of European philosophers coinciding in this respect with the greatest teacher of the greatest of Asiatic races and of a people who have never injured any one though many have injured them. There is, however, this apparent difference. The ideal Greek City as conceived by the Aryan philosophers was essentially warlike, every full citizen a perfectly trained warrior. Lao-Tse imagined his ideal State as surrounded by hosts of others similarly averse to aggression and conquest and exploitation. He could not bring himself even to think of such things as murder and rapine. "The multitudes of the heavenly hosts don't try to destroy each other. Why should you?"

Again, Aristotle would not imagine a City save with a God or Gods, their cult coming first and a very long way first. Lao-Tse has not a single word about religion at all, or even about death, save the bare commonplace:—

"It is no evil whatsoever, and probably the opposite of evil. You were born in order that you should die. Only foolish people and the vulgar will torment themselves about it."

We must never forget how their institution of slavery cramped and crippled the minds of those great Greek thinkers. It was so pervasive and pervading, so inter-penetrated every fibre of the body social that they could not even imagine it as non-existent, they could not even think themselves outside its power, just as our modern philosophers cannot think themselves outside of the power of money.

In Athens, in her prime and decline there were more than ten times as many slaves as free citizens. One man only—and a poor creature he was, Nicias, the commander of the Sicilian expedition—had a thousand slaves of his own working for him in the silver mines of Laurium. Another private citizen had 600. After the battle of Chaeronea an Athenian statesman proposed to enfranchise and arm 150,000 slaves; another sign of the vast populations which those little Greek territories were able to sustain. In order to retain in slavery such multitudes of men, men often quite as brave as themselves, it was necessary for all the free citizens of those antique States to be soldiers and at all moments ready with their weapons for the suppression of internal revolt: also to be gaolers and executioners and never to know genuine tranquillity of mind.

TEN.

GREEK WOMEN.

The great historic Greek men are tame, colourless, and uninteresting, compared with the passionately self-willed, self-directed Greek Men Gods and Demi-Gods of those prehistoric ages which are reflected in the surviving Epics and in the traditions founded upon the Epics. They were good citizens, virtuous, brave and honourable civic men and patriots, but in spite of all Plutarch's laudations and the consenting historians' murmur of applause, human interest in them, at the best, is languid. All their individual distinctive life was sucked out of them by the Polis, oligarchical or democratic, to which they belonged. They seem to have had hardly any more originality and individuality than the socialistic and communistic bee. As the bee is lost in her hive so the great historic Greek was lost in his Polis. The Polis owned him almost as much as it did the State slaves.

Take the very best of them, Pericles, statesman, orator, and philosopher. You find him seeming master, yet real servant of the Athenian Demos, chained to that service like the galley-slave to his oar.

When men consent to live indoors for any purpose what-soever it means an abnegation of their manhood. Towards the end of his life Pericles said: "The only road in all Greece that I know well is the road leading from my house to the Chambers where I conduct the affairs of the Athenians." That is, he led voluntarily the life of a clerk. He conducted, indeed, the affairs of the great Athenian Empire but the great

Athenian Empire was at the time really run by the merchants usurers and slave-driving manufacturers of the Peiraeus, to whom the Athenian Empire meant nothing but the profitable exploitation by themselves of all its constituent Cities and Islands. Demos at its worst had the great Pericles in thrall, and drove him into his office every day as it might a bought slave.

I use measured language, and speak by the book. When that Periclean Athenian Empire was at its highest height and Athens the greatest power on earth, the Chians made an appeal to the Athenians, grounding their appeal on considerations of clear justice. "Fear the Gods, O men of Athens," they said, "and do us this Justice."

"There is no such thing," replied the Athenians; "there is nothing but strength. We are stronger than you, and, justice or no justice, you must submit, and do what we tell you to do. And that is something in our interest and not in yours, O men of Chios."

This was the greatest crime known to the Greeks. They called it ὕβρις. And, where ὕβρις comes, the Erinnues, the Furies, are not far behind.

To create such an Empire for the use and behoof of the most blackguardly section of his people the noble Pericles for thirty years lived indoors, like a clerk, writing letters, framing treaties, dictating dispatches. And they were all much the same, the great historic Greeks, the colourless tame slaves of the Polis: Miltiades, Themistocles, Pelopidas, Demosthenes, Phocion, Aratus of Sicyon, Philopoemen, said to be the "Last of the Greeks." The Polis, grown corrupt, had tamed them, tamed them all. Before the Polis, democratic or oligarchical, the bravest of them, whether statesman or warrior, or both, like Epaminondas, did not dare even to call the nose upon his face his own.

Like the ant in the nest, the bee in the hive, the bravest of them became the helpless thralls of the vulgar aggregate, the Polis.

Aristides, for example, the typical Greek righteous man, so gave up to his Polis, that was Athens, everything that he had or had a right to have, that he left his children mendicants, and his grandchildren exhibiting tricks and charms around Athens for a living.

And, as to the Greek historic women—literally there are none, if we except Aspasia, only a few notorious prostitutes like Phryne, Lais and Theodota; none at all to set off against that grand procession of women and girls of the prehistoric Greek, when the great race was in its flush and bloom and pride, and flinging forth types with a prodigality like Nature's.

All the known types of Greek womanhood derive from pre-historic times, that is from the age of tiny monarchies when the King knew all his subjects, and the subject knocked at the palace door and said to the maid who opened, "I wish to see the King", the age of independent villages each in the midst of its own deme or village territory, and of friendly confederacies of adjoining villages, from the age of patriarchal clans when every Greek, though as a warrior second to none on the face of the earth, yet hated war as he hated death, pain and penury, when the slave was a member of the Family, and the Nation a more enlarged and more happy Family, when boys and girls were steeped in the spirit of poetry and religion yet innocent of letters, when the Greek Nations lived in the open air and the sunlight, before labour had begun to be a sorrow by becoming servile and forced, when property was hardly understood because the Gods owned all things and because "between friends there is no property". Such, in a considerable degree, was that Old Greece which we seem to see fading away with the emergence of the historic period. And it is out of that Old Greece so virtuous, pious, happy and free, have come down to us all those types of Greek womanhood and girlhood which appeal so powerfully even to-day to the heart and imagination of the modern European man, though the vast literature in which they were enshrined has been nearly wholly lost.

Recall Heré the beautiful bride, chaste mother, gracious, kindly, hospitable; the august queen of the household. What millions of Greek Herés tenderly and reverentially observed by the Poets, the Makers, as they went through Greece and the Islands observing considering and absorbing—what millions of such Greek household queens went to the creation of their Queen of Heaven and wife of Zeus supreme. All that was good, brave, beautiful in the Greek emerged out of his Herés, was suckled upon their deep breasts. We are so apt to forget that the men of Marathon, Salamis, Plataea, and the men who had the Persian at his peril not dare come within a hundred miles of the Asiatic Greek Cities were, all of them, once little helpless infants on the breasts of Greek mothers.

Recall Athené, the brave wise spinster, the proud beauty who would not mate, for reasons, yet taught little children tenderly and gave prudent counsel to men; an everlasting type; Artemis the good comrade, the fiercely chaste, with her *noli me tangere*;[59] nay, with her *timeto me tangere*,[60] roamer of the heathery mountains, lover of the beautiful wild things of the hillside and the forest; Hebé in the dewey bloom of her rosy youth; whoever else fails, the Hebés do not: they are always with us, like the Springs and the Dawns: Atalanta of Calydon collecting her heroes by the might of her beauty and her chastity, directing them upon the chase and destruction of monsters; Aphrodyte, sheer woman, what else can I say? Terrible as an army with banners: Medea touching the super-natural, controlling and directing forces and powers not human; Ariadné supporting the failing heroes lifting them on to victory; Omphalé with the hero at her feet meek and tame as a spaniel; the Erinnues, the Furies, the punishers, the aven-gers, here for ever, and thank God for that: beautiful Ceres crowned with wheat and her dread daughter, Persephoné, and her lovely daughter of the green springing corn, Koré, the damsel; Andromaché, with her baby on her breast, laughing and crying at the same time and Penelopé, true wives for ever; Nausicaa, princess-like and maidenly; Briseis, the affectionate grateful slave-girl. I only mention a few. In the vast Greek Epic cycle, now lost, known to us only from late Greeks who could only echo the echoes of the echoes of the great lost Epics, such names survive.

Authentic Greek history knows no such feminine types at all, only a few Phrynes better forgotten.

What do we gather from this? That the great age of the Greeks was pre-historic, that the Greeks, in respect to their women, as well as their men, began to fail and fade as they emerged into what we call History.

And this is exactly what we ought to expect, for History, the poor snob, follows always eloquently and admiringly in the track of strong crime, of successful rapine, of tyranny and slavery, of slaughter on a great scale, and is, perhaps necessarily, dumb concerning the ages of virtue and innocence and simple piety and goodness and kindly friendly inter-tribal relations, those of clan with clan, village with village, deme with deme.

For indeed the task of telling such a story is physically beyond her power, apart from her inherent aversion to innocence and her servile admiration for all violence inhumanity and crime. In the great age of the Greeks Attica alone consisted of near a hundred independent small Nations, Demes, villages with their territories. How could Dame History, putting her best foot forward and using her utmost industry—and we know that, at a pinch, she can be frightfully industrious—how could Dame Clio tell the story of a hundred Sovereign States? Impossible.

Now, there were, at this time, that is in the great age of the Greeks, the centuries of the expansion, thousands of such Greek States continental and insular. To tell their separate stories was altogether beyond her power. Therefore she had to wait until, here and there, through Confederation and concentration and through violence, conquest, and exploitation, strong criminal Powers emerged, and got into conflict with other strong criminal Powers. At such a point Dame History generally wakes up and begins to be alert, animated and eloquent. Strong crime emerges, the robber Kings of Assyria, the tyrant Empire of Athens, the man-slaying power of Rome and, with the robber thief and murderer, their applauder and kept flatterer, History emerges too and announces, not the end of the reign of innocence, but the beginning of Civilisation!

Happy the Nations that have no History. Unhappy and thrice unhappy the Nations concerning whom History is eloquent; for she is only eloquent and can by her nature be only eloquent concerning the crime.

"But, if that elder Greece was as innocent, pious and virtuous as you say, how comes it that their Epic Cycle contains too so much crime; horrible Thyestean banquets, rapes, murders, adulteries, incests? Surely the people who loved such stories cannot have been quite as good as gold".

A very fair question, which I shall consider more at large when I come to explain the disruption of the primeval Commune. Meantime you will observe that, even to-day, millions of virtuous, innocent, well-principled and well-conducted people do take a strange delight in crimes and horrors and things devilish. Their own lives are so tame and uneventful that they seem to need some such an escape. Hell itself was created and maintained in a flourishing condition for the very same reason.

That Greek age of innocence dimly revealed to us was not the Age of Gold, if such there ever was, but the Age of Silver. Life was innocent but also tame, slow and dull, and the Greek imagination demanded an escape. When we live again as Nature meant that we should live there will be no such un-Natural divorce between Life and Imagination, between Imagination and Actuality. Life will exhibit the boundless liberty of Imagination and Imagination the sanity which springs from the actualities, realities, positive knowledge and the experiences of Life. Modest girls don't want to hear of sensational adulteries or good-natured lads share imaginatively in the slaughter of poor savages or lucky findings of treasure. Nor will our good people torment and excite themselves about Hell and the Devil and the Judge. And for the present let this answer suffice.

ELEVEN.

A PICTURE.

NOT YET HAD MEN HEARD THE WAR-TRUMPET BLOWN, NOT YET
THE RINGING OF WOODS FORGED UPON HARD ANVILS.——VERGIL

Whence came the Aryans?

No one knows. No one really knows. They emerged upon the world some where, some how; young, fresh, vital, believing, hoping, full of faith. But from their fecund loins have sprung what mighty races!

I think myself that they first emerged, few in numbers, perhaps a single family or little group of friends, coming forth as the escapees of some pre-historic corrupt civilisation whose every monument has perished.

Lately while studying Sir H. Mayne's "Village Communes" and "Early European Institutions"[61] a friend presented me with a volume of Max Müller's translation of the Rig Vedas.

While reading these ancient delightfully fresh and vital hymns of early Aryans a picture grew upon my mind which entertained and amused myself for a while and which, translated into words, may possibly entertain and amuse others.

Necdum etiam audierant inflari classica necdum
Impositos duris creptiare incudibus enses.[62]

Grey dawn, hardly yet distinguishable from the waning night, nevertheless some abounding and multitudinous life is awake and astir here though night still lingers. A tumult of sounds innumerable fills the air; the glad shoutings and laughter of hosts of children penetrated by the strong ringing voices of men, the clear musical tones of women; barking of dogs, neighing and whinnying of horses, lowing of cows and bleating of sheep. The skylark is shrilling on high unseen. The early crow flies croaking through the dim air. Faint in the distance cries of wild animals are heard, unknown fauna of an unknown land. Scents of the damp and fragrant earth, of dewy grass and opening flowers fill the air.

Gradually a City reveals itself as darkness dislimns; a widespread City, unwalled, far lying, a City through which, as it were, the country flows; for indeed, it is a City of Cities, an irregular aggregation of hamlets, each hamlet well disjoined from the rest. The houses are low, white, and glistening, with brown roofs. In every hamlet stands one house larger than the rest; in the central hamlet one of considerable size, quadrangular, surrounded with pillars.

Outlines become more distinct, for the waste night has at last been effectually captured by the dawn.

All around are orchards of apple trees, plum trees, many kinds of fruit-bearing trees familiar or unknown; the fruit just now maturing or matured, for the time is late Summer. Everywhere gardens of flowers and of what seem to be roots and vegetables—here and there rows of beehives in sheltered places; rows of vines with their supports. Gold and tawny hues here and there on the leaves of all trees: further away fields of ripening corn.

But the ear asserts its rights against the eye; such is the increasing human uproar, especially the glad shoutings and cries of the seemingly human uproar, especially the glad shoutings and cries of the seemingly overwhelming juvenile population. From every hamlet they pour out in white streams, for indeed these children seem to be clad in some soft cream-coloured stuff. Like bees they pour forth shouting and singing into the orchards and gardens where they settle like flocks of birds stilling their noises for a while as they settle down to work there. Every child seems to know what it has to do. Women move amongst them to and fro, smilingly directing, smilingly chiding. Little boys mount into the branches of apple-trees and carefully drop the apples into the out-spread aprons of little girls upon the ground. Urchins driving toy wheel-barrows before them filled with rosy or golden apples are making for the City, one after the other, shouting. Huge industrial commotion reigns here, and unrestrained noise.

In the City men and women move to and fro or stand at their doors: they cry morning greetings to each other with clear glad voices. They are straight and tall, noble-looking, handsome or beautiful, all of them: very fair, though all faces seem bronzed from wind, air and sunshine. They are yellow-haired or fair-haired for the most part; a very fair race and with luminous faces. There are many old people, some seemingly of very great age. The old men are stately and majestic, very tranquil, nobler looking by far than the young men; the old women are more beautiful than the young.

The very old people, and the very young, the riotously glad and merry and pretty children, are the chief ornaments of the City.

All, both men and women, wear their hair long and at its full natural length, but the women and girls half veil theirs. The veils, of a sheeny white, fall from the middle of the crown and flow down behind them. Of trinkets and much-like ornaments they appear to be quite innocent.

On the east some nine miles distant a dimly gleaming sea extends to the horizon; Cities of grouped hamlets show white on the sea-shore. In the uplands towards the south-east, half-hidden in forest, there is another. From each City tall expanding pillars of smoke show dim against gleaming wave and green hill side.

There is here plainly a federal group, a confraternity of rural republics. No one here carries weapons; no face shows signs of fear or care or anger.

From the uplands two streams descending unite hard by on the left and run together to the sea. Children are playing and paddling there, catching stickle-backs, building bridges, doing one knows not what, doing what it has been the custom of children to do with running streams ever since the beginning of time, and ever will be.

"We twa hae paidled i' the burn
Frae morning sun till dine."[63]

A sudden thunder of many hoofs and a herd of eager horses gallop from the camp; on the back of every horse a little white animated figure; little boys riding the big horses to water.

On all sides great yellow fields of corn, further off pastures with cattle amongst whom girls move to and fro with their pails, singing: true *daughters** of the republic.

One whole quarter of the City seems given over to industry and handicrafts. Here arise the sounds of hammering on timber, of sawing, the wild whistle of the Carpenter's plane, the ringing of the smith's hammer on the anvil and the husky breath of his bellows. Workshops of all kinds abound in this quarter. The potter shapes his shapeless clay, as his wheel runs merrily round; the weaver bends to right and left as he shoots the willing shuttle from side to side and sings one of the songs peculiar to his craft, a song which is also a hymn, also a prayer. His loom and his shuttle are to him not dead instruments of production but the outward shape and form of an invisible beneficent intelligence. Every one sings, for to every one his work is lovely and pleasant; it gladdens him. He worships and loves the instruments of his craft, worships and loves the mystic presences within them which he senses though he sees not. So too, the wheel-right works, and the tailor, here a full man, as good as the best, and better; stitching here, glad, proud and happy in the dawn—in the dawn.

The workshops lie all open. We can see the men at their work. Here in the open air strong boys and young men drive swiftly round the long projecting turning-bars of a mill. Singing they speed the revolution of the great upper mill stone. They have frames and muscles as of steel and knotted whipcord; their white calves bulge out as they pass, gripping the ground

---

* O'Grady's note: The Sanskrit word from which our "daughter" is derived means the milker.

with strong feet. They sing for the corn god; nay, shout; full of youth and hope and vitality and bravery and inexhaustible strength and power; young Samsons; but unblinded; not disillusioned and not slaves. Free; they never knew, never will know, what it feels like to look into the eyes of a tyrant or accept the wages of slavery.

They can see, every time they come round, the torrent of white flour pouring from the dark gut in the nether mill stone and the great growing pyramid forming on the linen cloth beneath. Their mothers and sisters will bake it into good bread to feed the strength of the republic.

This quarter is alive and loud with industry, happy industry, with the noise of craftsmen and their pupils engaged in scores of beautiful creative occupations, the glad labour of making, of creating.

In a pillared shed sits a shoe or sandal-maker thoughtfully pointing his lastend with a bristle. He turns his eyes now and then with a gentle expression upon a little boy of four who sits beside him wearing a small leathern apron, vigorously hammering a bit of leather upon a lap-stone and changing the hammer from hand to hand, as either hand grows tired. Indeed children seem to be about everywhere in these quarters intermingling with the men and welcomed by them; very industrious too and imitating the work of their seniors with toy instruments.

The shoe or sandal-maker is an intellectual-looking young man. Sometimes his eyes wear a far away expression for indeed he is a poet too and the favourite poet of the clan. He is revolving now some neater cadence or telling phrase as he sits and works at his bench and smiles at his little four years old friend and admirer. What a strange City! All so clean too; its people all so busy, strenuously busy, happily so while the dew is still on the ground and the sun unrisen.

Now strong voices of command sound from that great quadrangular building in the City's centre, and from its wide doors stream forth continually torrents of untamed humanity; men and lads who disappear swiftly in different directions fulfilling the commands of their elders.

Hark! The baying of hounds. From the same building rushes forth a troop of running youths succinctly clad each with a huge hound straining before him, held back by a leash. They carry spears. On their backs they wear quivers filled with arrows, and bows fastened transversely from shoulder to thigh. One bears a great net rolled up on his shoulders and concealing his head. They are all young and swift, bright and brave and glad.

From another door stride forth a score of youths bearing axes which they hold upright before them, and march past us to the South, looking at the shining axe-heads and singing together some sonorous song as they march.

It is a hymn to the axe, to the friendly bright potent one who lives in the axe.

So they march through and out of the City to the woods and the sound of their singing grows faint in the distance.

Still the dawn brightens and all things grow clearer, radiant Ushas, the immortal, the daily born, now revealing all her beauty. Eastward, beyond other far-scattered white Cities resembling ours rise mountains clad with great forests still in shadow, and beyond them again very, very far away, rosy pinnacles of snow above which clouds full-filled with the dawn gorgeously reflect the face of the coming Sun. O Suryas, enlightener, O Savitar, lord of light and life, surely thou art at hand![64]

Hark! a clash of loud cymbals followed by the strains of stringed instruments and, as if with one impulse the whole population converging from everywhere stream in crowds through its ways and pour forth upon a spacious lawn all with their lit faces towards the dawn, old men and women, young men and women, boys and girls and that host of children, mothers leading the very little children or bearing infants on their breasts.

All the children carry in their hands pitchers made of some shining white substance, a pitcher or vase in either hand. The very little children too have theirs, even many infants in their mothers' arms have been taught to bear carefully their little vessels. Every face is radiant with gladness, illuminated with some rare enthusiasm.

On the green lawn they form in long ranks, rank behind rank. In the first line stand the smallest children and the mothers with infants. All stand for a while motionless and silent, gazing eastward at the glowing clouds, the ruddy golden seas of brightness poured over those far off peaks of snow.

One young man in no way distinguishable from the rest— no priest but just a selected chief sacrificer or, may be volunteer, raises with both hands above his head a shining pitcher and pours forth before him what appears to be a stream of milk. It is really a mingled stream of milk and the intoxicating juice of the Soma plant.[65] He has no altar other than the green grass.

Now, all at once, the people break forth into singing: a song in an unknown tongue which may be translated, has been translated, into ours, thus; into our less liquid-flowing language, a poor substitute for that divine speech.[66]

SONG AT SUNRISE

Thou art invited to this innocent fair sacrifice of milk-offering:
>   With thy Maruts come hither, O Agni.
No god or man is mightier than thou, O mighty one;
>   With thy Maruts come hither, O Agni.
With the bright divine host void of guile:
>   With those Maruts come hither, O Agni.
The mighty ones, unconquerable by strength; shouting their songs.
>   With those Maruts come hither, O Agni.
The shining ones, holding terrible purposes, very strong,
>   consumers of their enemies:
>   With the Maruts come hither, O Agni.
Whose thrones, as of gods, are in the heavens,
>   Yea, in the lights of the firmament;
>   With the Maruts come hither, O Agni.
Who whirl the clouds mightily across the raging seas;
>   With the Maruts come hither, O Agni.

Whose arrows are the lightnings that they dart across the sea;
  With the Maruts come hither, O Agni.
For whom we have poured forth the early draught, milk and sweet Soma,
  With the Maruts come hither, O Agni.

Again silence, but only for a few seconds for now the great red sun suddenly lifts himself, nay, springs, leaps as with a fiery spring from the snowy horizon.

At the welcome sign announcing manifestly the return of that dear friend, all raise on high their arms and hands above their heads, even the infants in the mothers' arms being taught to raise theirs too, and then, slowly lowering them as they bend forward, they touch the ground and again stand as before. This is done seven times after which one great shout of welcome, great voices and little voices all mingling in one glad triumphant cry, and the simple heart-felt liturgy and matin service are at an end.

The strong and faithful one, father and friend and giver of all good things has duly returned to his children and has been duly welcomed and honoured; he, visible, with his host of invisible Maruts, the wild self-born Maruts, some times clad in storms and scattering lightenings, sometimes shedders of the good rain, but now radiant and joyful, the attending host that surrounds and accompanies the journeying of the sun through the great vault of heaven.

"A simple religion." Yes a simple religion truly, the simple religion of our far, far away Aryan sires.

Have we not travelled a good way since then and has it been up? or down?

This was our Aryan state of innocence, the *Saturnia Regna*[67] of which the Romans, even in their corruptions, hold still some sure though indistinct memory.

It was a savage state, in a sense; many of the luxuries enjoyed by us in our great modern Cities and amid our advanced civilisation were not to be had there. Yet, such as it was, it was at least happy; happy and innocent. How did we fall from that state? By what way and how did the Devil steal into this primitive Eden? Or, rather, how did he rise up within it? For sure we may be that he is here somewhere; somewhere?

Let us look again some thousand or even thousands of years later, and see what we shall see. Our City is all changed and quite unrecognisable. It is small and surrounded by a great earthen rampart palisaded and fossed. A sluice from that stream feeds the foss.

The houses are massed together; there are no green spaces. Everything seems less luminous than of yore. The people are dressed in sadder-coloured raiment, though many wear barbaric ornaments. Armed men with hard faces move to and fro.

The mill is here still driven by a gang of men who go round less rapidly and with more of labour and of strain, though an overseer with a whip stands by and sometimes plies it, while he threatens and roars. From the fields men come into the city and arm themselves, but many remain in the fields working, overseers on horseback are there armed and cracking whips. There is a public assembly of all the armed men. From it arise vociferations and angry shoutings.

Who are the men who drive the mill and remain working in the fields?

Slaves.

The Slave has come in, and with him the tyrant, and in our innocent rural republic of all the virtues, joys and delights of a simple yet sufficient life the evil principle has asserted itself and the Devil broken loose.

The slave has come in; and the tyrant; the man unarmed who labours and the man armed who labours not but will flog that other if slow to labour, will pursue him with dogs if he flies, kill him if he rebels; and the fraternity and freedom of our little rural Aryan commonwealth are at an end.

I have painted a full length picture of that little State, I will not paint a full length picture of this.

Evil is strengthened by being talked about. Only I note before we pass that there is a religious ceremony forward where, in strange garments, a priest officiates at an altar and where the offering is no longer milk and Soma but a reluctant ox dragged forcibly by ropes to the altar, whose forehead that strong priest cleaves with a pole axe.[68]

*Procumbit Humi bos**

The gods now worshipped look for blood.

Classes, orders, castes have been evolving and differentiating here, a priestly class, an aristocratic class, a slave class. Presently there will be a quite leisured class, people living upon slave labour and doing nothing; and, under all, supporting all, feeding, housing, clothing all, the slave, under fed, ill housed, ill clothed, working hard, very hard, under the lash, under menace of death, divorced from his freedom, from his manhood.

Amongst its other varied and manifold intellectual offspring civilisation has produced its own historians who naturally are loyal to their sire. They tell us—See Harmsworth's History of the World[69]—they tell us—they make no secret of it, that Civilisation began with the slave.

He made the leisured class and the leisured class made Civilisation.

The world's historians tell us this quite frankly, and are not ashamed of it.

---

*O'Grady's note: On the ground the ox falls. Vergil [*Aeneid* v: 481].

NOTES.

1   Probably quoted from Robert Burton (1576–1640), quoting Giraldus Cambrensis in *Camden's Remains*. O'Grady leaves out the beginning of the epigram: "Mira cano": "Wonders I sing". The quoted part translates: "The sun has set; no night has followed."

2   The crocus sativus, saffron in colour, was used in depiction of gods as early as *c.* 1500 BC in Minoan Crete. It was later given Christian meanings.

3   Ovid, *Metamorphoses,* Book 1, ll. 85–6. Translation: "He gave man an uplifted countenance, with the order to gaze up to Heaven and, upright, to raise the face to the stars."

4   A missing chapter with this title belongs here. Only the title page survives.

5   Charles Fourier (1772–1837), French, anti-industrial, utopian socialist.

6   Poem no. 32 in *Song of Myself.* The full passage reads:
    I think I could turn and live with animals, they are so placid and
        self-contained,
    I stand and look at them long and long.
    They do not sweat and whine about their condition,
    They do not lie awake in the dark and weep for their sins,
    They do not make me sick discussing their duty to God,
    Not one is dissatisfied, not one is demented with the mania of
        owning things,
    Not one kneels to another, nor to his kind that lived thousands of
        years ago,
    Not one is respectable or unhappy over the whole earth.

7   "Intimations of Immortality from Recollections of Early Childhood" (1807).

8   William Blake, "Auguries of Innocence" (First published 1863).

9   Robert Burns, "To a Mouse, on Turning Her Up in Her Nest with the Plough" (1785).

10   Robert Burns, "For A' That" (1795). The lines read:
                    For a' that an' a' that,
        It's coming yet for a' that,—
                That man to man, the world o'er,
        Shall brothers be for a' that!

11   John Ruskin (1819–1900), most prominent Victorian art critic.

12   *Anni fugaces*: fleeing years. *Libitina*: the goddess of corpses.

13   John 3: 7.

14 John Keats, "Ode to a Nightingale" (1820).

15 Robert Burns, "Song—The Rigs o' Barley" (1783).

16 Robert Burns, "To a Mouse, on Turning Her Up in Her Nest with the Plough" (1785).

17 The typescript apparently continued here but is missing.

18 Ralph Johnson, *The Scholar's Guide.* 1665; rpt Scolar Press, 1971: "The Latin tongue loves Verbals, Participials, Gerundives, and Participles of the future in rus."

19 John Dryden, "A Song for St Cecilia's Day" (1687).

20 "Invocation" (1824).

21 O'Grady is right: "sym-" means "together"; "bolon" is a variant of the word meaning "throw".

22 Sir William Mitchell Ramsay (1851–1939), prolific author of numerous books on Greek civilisation, the early Christian Church, and Asia Minor.

23 William Wordsworth. "Lines Written a Few Miles above Tintern Abbey" (1798). Lines 123–4 actually read: "Knowing that Nature never did betray/The heart that loved her . . .".

24 O'Grady is alluding to the Inquisition, and the passage seems to have a primarily Catholic audience in mind as the reference to St Francis of Assisi might suggest.

25 Matthew 11: 30.

26 2 Samuel 5: 24.

27 Fragment 92.

28 Much of the following chapter was published previously. A version appeared in the Christmas number of *The Irish Worker* in 1912—republished in *To the Leaders of Our Working People* (Dublin: University College Dublin Press, 2002); a second version, found with the typescript of *Sun and Wind*, was published under the title "Sun and Wind" in A. R. Orage's *The New Age*, 3 July 1913, pp. 261–3. Passages omitted in the *Sun and Wind* typescript but published in *The New Age* are included here in italics.

29 Isaiah 52: 7.

30 Genesis 27: 27.

31 James Anthony Froude (1818–95). Many similar sentiments are expressed in his three-volume *The English in Ireland in the Eighteenth Century* (1872–4).

32 Francis Dobbs (1750–1811). The speech here referred to was delivered 7 June 1800.

33 O'Grady here echoes the anti-Catholic Article 31 of the 39 Articles of the Church of England. Article 31 reads in part: "Wherefore the sacrifices of Masses, in the which it was commonly said that the priests did offer Christ for the quick and the dead to have remission of pain or guilt, were *blasphemous fables and dangerous deceits*."

34 Apparently a reference to Christiaan Rudolf de Wet (1854–1922),

Boer soldier and statesman, famous for miraculous escapes from British forces during the Boer War.

35 Edward Walford, Tr. *The Politics and Economics of Aristotle* (London, 1866).

36 Thomas Campbell (1777–1844), "Ye Mariners of England" (*c.* 1800).

37 George Grote (1794–1871), *A History of Greece.* 12 vols (1846–57).

38 Deuteronomy 27: 17.

39 Psalms 133: 1.

40 Isaiah 52: 7.

41 Matthew 5: 9.

42 O'Grady seems to have slipped here and reversed the historical order.

43 Aristotle, *The Politics.* Book IV.

44 Mercenary soldiers.

45 John Lempriere (*c.*1765–1824), *Bibliotheca Classica or Classical Dictionary* (1788), a source of questionable quality.

46 Judges 17: 6.

47 Genesis 8: 11.

48 A version of this chapter appeared under this title in *The Irish Review*, 1 (1911), 161–4.

49 Thomas Carlyle, *History of Friedrich II of Prussia*, Book XXI, "Afternoon and Evening of Friedrich's Life, 1763–1786". Chapter 1, "Prefatory".

50 Annexed to the manor, i.e., they could not be sold apart from the manor but could be conveyed with the manor upon its sale.

51 J. B. Bury, *A History of Greece.* Modern Library first edition: 1900.

52 Robert Burns, "To a Haggis" (1786).

53 This chapter appeared in the September 1911 issue of *The Irish Review*, pp. 313–21.

54 O'Grady misquotes Byron's "The Isles of Greece" slightly: "Suli's steep" should be "Suli's rock," and "here" should be "there."

55 *Paradise Lost.* Book I, l. 549.

56 Translation: "the hungry Greek". Juvenal, *Satires* 3:76.

57 O'Grady may be referring to Col. Thomas Sadlier, who, as governor of Galway under Cromwell, was charged with emptying the city of all Papists in 1659.

58 Tribes that founded Rome.

59 Translation: touch me not. John 20:17.

60 Translation: fear to touch me.

61 Sir Henry Summer Maine (1822–88), *Lectures on the Early History of Institutions* (1888).

62 Vergil, *Georgics II*: 539–40. Translation: "nor yet had they heard war-trumpets blown, nor yet the hard anvil clink under the sword".

63 Robert Burns, "Auld Lang Syne" (1796).

64 Various names for the sun in the Rig Vedas.

65 The haoma plant, a leafless vine of eastern India, yielding a sour, milky juice. In Zoroastrianism, a sacramental drink prepared with the juice of the haoma plant, milk, and water.

66 Sanskrit or the putative, original tongue of the Aryans.

67 The Saturnian Age when Astraea, the Goddess of Justice, reigned in the Golden Age.

68 Ox sacrifice was common among the Anglo-Saxons—the subject of a letter by Pope Gregory in 601.

69 Published 1907.